THE FUNCTION

OF CRITICISM

Problems and Exercises

BY

YVOR WINTERS

ALAN SWALLOW, *Denver*

801
W73f
71139
September, 1970

Copyright 1957 by Yvor Winters

Printed in the United States of America

SECOND EDITION

To J. V. CUNNINGHAM

*Whose work in prose and in verse alike
has been more valuable to me
than that of any other writer of our time*

The first essay in this book was published in *The Hudson Review,* in the Autumn issue of 1956. The second was published in *The Hudson Review* in the Autumn of 1951. The third was published in *The Hudson Review* in two issues: Winter, 1949, and Spring, 1949. The fourth was published in *The Sewanee Review* in the Autumn of 1948. The last was published in *The Hudson Review* in the Summer of 1955. I wish to express my obligation to the editors of *The Hudson Review* and of *The Sewanee Review.* Since the essays are not published in chronological order, the reader should observe the dates, if the chronological order happens to interest him.

The essay on Hopkins was delivered in the form of two public lectures, sponsored by *The Hudson Review,* at Princeton University in the spring of 1948. The essay entitled The Audible Reading of Poetry was delivered as a single public lecture at the Kenyon School of English, Kenyon College, in the summer of 1949. Both essays have since been enlarged and otherwise modified.

Contents

Problems

for the Modern Critic

of Literature

I.

The first problem with which the critic of literature is confronted is to find a mode of living which will enable him to develop his mind, practice his art, and support his family. The universities offer the obvious solution, but the matter is worth at least brief discussion.

The universities as we know them today are of relatively recent growth, in this country certainly, and in a large measure abroad; they have developed during a period in which romantic ideas about literature have flourished. Literature has been regarded in this period as essentially an "expression" of emotion, has been so regarded by poets, professors, and critics about equally, and consequently that is what it has been in the main; and poets and other writers have been expected to be temperamental and irresponsible and consequently have often been so; and a great many temperamental and irresponsible people, who in more fortunate ages would never have thought that they were artists, have been led to believe that their personal weaknesses were signs of genius. Thus the professors have made a living by what they have regarded as the serious study of literature; but the men who have composed the literature were not serious, in the professors' opinion and sometimes in fact, and hence have been considered unfit to study or teach it. Each group has traditionally held the other in contempt.

When I was young, I and my contemporaries thought of Irving Babbitt, a man who was thirty-five when I was born, as a Professor, and with some show of reason: he held the title at Harvard, he had obviously read a great deal, he was quite obviously imperceptive in writing about poetry, and he held a number of ideas which might have been usable had he not simplified some and confused the others almost out of recognition. But for Babbitt's colleagues, Babbitt was a professor largely on sufferance: he was really a dangerous innovator. It was not that they had discovered the

11

weaknesses in his critical system, for to the best of my knowledge there is no evidence in print to show that they had, though they made many irrelevant objections to it.[1] The trouble was that he was a critic and had defended criticism as an academic discipline and had attacked the colleges and universities for neglecting it.

But for the young men of my generation, Babbitt was the Professor in person: the other professors were an indistinguishable crowd. And Babbitt had a way of saying stupid things about great poems: so we looked elsewhere for our enlightenment. We found our enlightenment in Ezra Pound. Pound had enough scholarship to impress the young, but it was largely linguistic. He was incapable of thought, and his theories of poetry were merely restatements of principles which had been flourishing for over two centuries: the corrosive principles of eighteenth-century sentimental-romanticism and associationism. But we were ignorant, and his principles, as he stated them, seemed new. Furthermore, he had two closely related gifts which Babbitt lacked: he could write poetry, which, however it might be damaged by his theories, showed a real genius for language; and he could show us poems and passages which were genuinely fine. He showed us fine poems which we had overlooked, whereas Babbitt all too often misunderstood fine poems with which we were familiar. For about fifteen years Pound was the most influential critic in American letters, so far as practical results were concerned; and when he was replaced, it was by his disciple Eliot, who did little save restate his ideas in a more genteel style. Pound's disciples in the main inherited his ideas without his talents—the usual procedure—and since the ideas were bad, the result was bad. Pound might have been a much more effective critic if he had been able to study under a first-rate historian of ideas; but there were almost none of these in Pound's day, and he broke with the university system over a stupid incident at a small middle-western college, and he attacked the system violently throughout the rest of his career.

Pound and Babbitt represent the traditional cleavage well enough, even though Babbitt's colleagues may have thought him rather far to the left. Each had natural gifts which the other lacked; neither was trained in the areas in which he was deficient.

12

Now I would not go so far as to say that training is a substitute for talent, but after twenty-odd years of teaching, I am convinced that teaching is possible, and that if a man is brilliant in some one intellectual department, it is usually possible to improve him— and to improve him a great deal—where he is weak. But if such teaching is to be done, it ordinarily must be done by a man who is at least passably competent in all of the areas in question. Twenty-five years ago such men were simply not available in the American universities, and had never been. Today there is a fair number of them. The change represents a revolution in the teaching of literature. During these years the quality of traditional scholarship has improved as well, and I believe that the improvement is due in a considerable measure to the critics on the faculties. I do not mean that the critics invariably have all the answers, but most of them at least know what some of the important questions are, and they stimulate thought and perception; and the result has been a degree of sophistication among the younger scholars of my time which I did not find in my elders, and the difference, I suspect, is more a difference of education than of native gift, though it is also true that some gifted men are now staying in the profession who a generation ago would have seen no future in it.[2]

The revolution was initiated, doubtless, by Babbitt; but a handful of men of my generation bore the brunt of it: Ransom, Tate, Brooks, Blackmur, and myself. The Chicago critics, a few of whom are older than any of the men just named, moved onto the scene somewhat later. I am proud of my part in this revolution, but my part was not an easy one. Of the four gentlemen who have been head of the department of English at Stanford in my time, the second, the late Professor A. G. Kennedy, told me that criticism and scholarship do not mix, that if I wanted to become a serious scholar I should give up criticism. He told me likewise that poetry and scholarship do not mix, and that he had given up writing poetry at the age of twenty-five. And he added that my publications were a disgrace to the department. Fortunately for myself, he was the only one of the four department heads to hold these views, but one was almost enough. And he was far from an exception so far as the profession as a whole was concerned. There were other men like him at Stanford, some in positions of greater power; and there were others like him elsewhere. At least two of the critics whom I have mentioned in connection with myself have had comparable experiences, and I have heard respectable scholars tell stories of boorish rudeness to or concerning one or two of these men, have heard them tell the stories as if the incidents were triumphs of the intellect or of humor or of both. A good deal of this kind of thing is due to ineradicable human jealousy; but a good deal of it is due to the traditional cleavage which I have mentioned, and in so far as it is due to this should become less active with time. But I and my critical associates are still something very like bohemians in the eyes of many of our colleagues. In fact the Chicago critics, all of whom were respectable historical scholars before they avowed their interest in criticism, have been looked on with a good deal of hostility by other scholars for some years, as if they were somehow renegades; and they in turn seem to regard all other critics, no matter what their degrees or academic positions, as unbaptized or worse.

But the Chicago group are technically professors, in spite of what other professors may have thought. My casual impression is that the Chicago group are somewhat more methodical scholars in the traditional forms of scholarship than are the so-called New Critics whom I have just mentioned, and are somewhat less talented in understanding works of literature. But the two groups have gotten close enough together so that they can—as such people go—understand each other to some extent whenever they are willing to make the effort. And they have actually crossed lines here and there: Mr. Elder Olson, one of the Chicagoans, has written a book praising one of the most naive romantics of our time, the late Dylan Thomas. I doubt—or let me say that I hope I may safely doubt—that any of my bohemian associates would be quite so innocent.

14

II

The scholars, in brief, have become more literary, even when they appear at times, like Professor Olson, to be sowing a belated crop of wild oats, and the literary men have become more scholarly, and both groups are in the universities; and this is a gain of the utmost importance, especially for the young men who are now taking advanced degrees in literature. But what are the other achievements of criticism in our time? What have the critics done besides asking important questions, propounding incomplete or untenable theories, attacking each other's theories, and defending their preferences for particular works? Besides irritating the older scholars to a modicum of thought and stimulating the graduate students of the country to more active thought about literature than we have ever witnessed before? Is it fair that we should ask more of them than this? I think it fair that we should ask more, and I think that they have done very little more.

If we are to have any kind of critical guidance, we shall have to have some kind of critcal method or methods that are really applicable to the business in hand. If we are to have any kind of critical method, we shall have to understand two topics with more or less clarity: the potentialities of different kinds of subject matter and the potentialities of various literary forms. Any understanding of these topics, in turn, will depend upon our view of the purpose, or final cause, of literature. In general, our critics have been afraid to commit themselves to any theory of a final cause, or if they suggest one have been afraid to state it clearly and to endeavor to implement it, and thus have been crippled from the start. The theories that have been offered will hardly endure inspection.

Let me illustrate.

I have written at length of T. S. Eliot and of John Crowe Ransom elsewhere. Both men have criticized individual poems and other works in more or less detail and hence have exposed themselves to attack in a way for which—if I may borrow a phrase from Mr. Ransom—I honor them. It is only by such criticism that we lay the groundwork for general theories; and the men who are willing to engage in such criticism have the courage of their convictions. Similar work has been performed by Tate, Brooks, and Blackmur. Many others have done such work, it goes without saying, but these are the men who have influenced our time more than any others. Eliot is an extremely contradictory theorist, but he appears to see literature as the expression of emotion and emotion as determined by the period: he is therefore a determinist, so far as literature is concerned, and what one might call an historical relativist, in spite of the fact that he does not really like the literature of the nineteenth century. Ransom is much more consistent, and, unlike Eliot, he endeavors to be consistent and to clarify his views, but his doctrine of imitation, from which he derives his doctrine of the logical core and the tissue of irrelevances, appears to be merely one more homespun theory in defense of the associational techniques developed in the eighteenth century. Eliot, a spiritual descendant of Pound, and Tate, whose ideas derive in part from Ransom and in part from Eliot, are deeply involved in related principles.

Brooks offers a theory of ironical opposition, or paradox, as a theory of poetic structure, a theory to which R. S. Crane has made some very sound objections.[3] The worst difficulty with Brooks's method, as we see it in operation, is this: that any poem in which he can detect the ironical or paradoxical structure—and he can detect it almost anywhere—appears to him excellent, and nothing except this structure appears, in his opinion, to be involved in the art of poetry. The stylistic defects of *The Canonization,* of the *Elegy Written in a Country Churchyard,* of the *Ode on the Intimations of Immortality,* of *Among Schoolchildren*—and the defects in these poems are many and serious—do not exist for him. The defects in the themes of these poems become virtues of method. And one of these poems is as good as another, and, so far as one can tell, as good as any other. Like Crane, he seems to see poetry purely as structure—in Brooks it is a kind of balance between thematic opposites—and not as a definable method of understanding human experience and judging it. He is inferior to Crane for the reason that Crane points out: he is aware of only one principle of structure and that one inadequate. He is superior to Crane in this: that he makes a serious attempt to explore the possibilities of his principle in the analyses of a good many poems. Neither man seems to be aware that the primary function of criticism is evaluation, and that unless criticism succeeds in providing a usable system of evaluation it is worth very little.

Blackmur appears to be unwilling to commit himself to any principles, but feels that all principles should be used as methods of exploration.[4] One never feels sure why they should be used, since we do not know in reading Blackmur what we are looking for, and we suspect that he is looking only for what he may happen to turn up. He appears to be a relativist, and a relativist in criticism is of little help to anyone save himself, and one would like to reserve the right to be sceptical about even that. I may be unjust to Blackmur, however, for he has neglected the arts of syntax and of organization to the point that it is almost impossible to understand him.

Allen Tate, in his volume *Reason in Madness*,[5] has published four essays which have some bearing on what I have to say. In the order in which they appear in the book, they are: *The Present Function of Criticism, Literature as Knowledge, Tension in Poetry*, and *Miss Emily and the Bibliographers*. The first and last of these are essentially attacks upon the professors of English, particularly those in the graduate schools; *Literature as Knowledge* is mainly an attack upon the semanticists. Let me say at once that I think the attack upon the semanticists is a very effective piece of work, though I think that if Tate had not troubled himself some one else would have done the work for him—in fact the work might well have been done merely by the normal ravages of time. As to the professors whom he attacks, they are not an illusion: they are the professors who engage in "serious" literary study—bibliography, philology, textual criticism, and related disciplines—in order to lay the groundwork for criticism, and who not only hold criticism in contempt but do their best to suppress it in the universities. I, too, have known them. They are less numerous now than they were when Tate was writing these essays; and their number is diminishing. These men were fools, and where they still flourish they are still fools; and they have ex-

17

erted a good deal of power in the past and doubtless still exert power in varying measures in various institutions. Yet even fifteen or twenty years ago they were a parody on the serious historical scholar, the scholar who engaged in factual investigation because the investigation was useful and his own real but limited talents lay in that direction. Tate gives the impression that his parody is the universal type, and this, I think, is unjust. It is, in fact, a blessing that the historical scholar has not as a rule engaged in criticism, for ordinarily he has no talent for it; and on the other hand Tate and I would both be far more ignorant men than we are if it had not been for his work: he has helped to educate us.

He has helped to educate us by doing his proper work, and we should help to educate him and his successors by doing ours, for the study of literature is extremely difficult, involves great and various ranges of learning, and will never be wholly mastered or clarified by any one man. Tate's final sentence in *The Present Function of Criticism* reads: "Literature is the complete knowledge of man's experience, and by knowledge I mean the unique and formed intelligence of the world of which man alone is capable." At the end of *Literature as Knowledge* he makes a similar statement. It is my contention that such a statement should have introduced an essay, and that the essay should then have explored the implications of the statement fully. Had Tate written such an essay, he would have been performing his proper function as a critic, a function which he blames the historical scholars for not having performed. Only once, so far as I can recollect, has Tate moved in the direction which I recommend, and neither I nor my ablest graduate students have succeeded in plotting the course of his motion.

I refer to his essay entitled *Tension in Poetry*. In this essay he employs the word *tension* to include the meanings of its two derivatives: *extension* and *intension*. *Extension* means denotation; *intension* means connotation. The ideal tension in a poem would be a maximum content of both. But what is a maximum here? Is there any functional relationship between the one and the other, is any propriety of relationship involved? Tate does not say. Like Arnold before him, he gives us a handful of touchstones:

passages of poetry which he likes, although he admits that some of them are not the greatest poetry, and which are notable mainly for the reason that they resemble each other in no very obvious way. If I were to come to this essay unprepared, I would suspect that Tate was indicating something like the relationship which I myself have endeavored to define between the motive (indicated most obviously in the denotative content of language) and the emotion (indicated most obviously in the connotative), and that he would demand a defensible relationship between the two. Yet Tate has told me in conversation that he regards my theory as indefensible philosophically, though useful as a tactical weapon. When I asked him to enlarge upon this statement, he declined. It is perhaps unfair to quote from conversation—in fact I am sure that it is—but this is a serious matter, and Tate has never given me any further satisfaction. If my breach of propriety stimulates Tate to an explanation, I shall be gratified and more than likely improved.

The leading figure in the Chicago group is R. S. Crane, and he is one of the few living critics who have endeavored to define any kind of critical method. It is impossible not to feel a good deal of sympathy for Crane: he is definitely a man at work. The central weakness in Crane's thought, however, is the same as that in the thought of so many of the others: a refusal to define any final cause for poetry other than the perfection of its own form—whatever that may mean. He sometimes appears to believe that there is, or sometimes may be, a relationship between poetry and moral judgment; more often he informs us that poetry, or at any rate poetic tragedy, gives us pleasure because it awakens and then allays strong emotions. But he does not pursue either topic. He does not tell us whether all poetry has moral value, or, if not, how some poetry differs from other poetry in this respect; nor does he tell us why strong emotions should be either awakened or allayed, nor what the relationship may be between either of these phenomena and any poetic technique. He offers no concept of propriety of emotion in a given context, or what I have called elsewhere a just relationship of emotion to motive, but seems to see the awakening of strong emotion as a good in itself, and he could

19

thus be used effectively by the most irresponsible of romantic theorists. He insists on the importance of studying the various literary forms, their subdivisions and aspects, in order that we may understand the principles governing them, and in this I believe he is right. I believe furthermore that the pages in which he recommends this kind of study are among the most intelligent and persuasive of our time. Yet there seems to be no consistent awareness in his remarks that the most important end of such study would be the establishment of some kind of hierarchy of potentialities among the various forms, their subdivisions, and their elements; nor that the establishment of any such hierarchy would be impossible unless we had a clear idea of what the final cause of literature should be, so that we could evaluate the different forms in relationship to this cause; nor that we would have, in fact, no basis for saying that a given work was an admirable example of its kind, unless we could see the kind as a related division of the whole.

Yet back of his unwillingness to commit himself on this subject, there lurks an habitual and emotional commitment to the traditional order of forms: tragedy, epic, and lyric (with comedy, perhaps, tucked away in a footnote) ; and there lurks the undefended belief that "imitation," in the sense in which Crane derives this term from Aristotle, is the highest form of art. His derivation and definition of the term are sound, so far as my limited scholarship will permit me to judge. Yet nowhere does he tell us why imitation is important, except to say that it affords us a particular pleasure through awakening and allaying our emotions. If we were to tell him that we prefer to keep our emotions allayed from the beginning, there is nothing, I believe, in his system, which would provide him with the materials of an answer. At no point in his published works, so far as I can recollect, does he even make a comparison between the mimetic method and the expository method, with reference to their potentialities: there is the almost invariable assumption that the mimetic method is somehow the essentially poetic, and that other methods, though possible and defensible, are subsidiary.

This preference shows itself in his remarks on Gray's *Elegy*, remarks repeated in *The Languages of Criticism and the Structure of Poetry* from his earlier essay on Cleanth Brooks. He asks us to regard the *Elegy* as an "imitative lyric of moral choice rather than of action or of mood, representing a situation in which a virtuous, sensitive, and ambitious young man of undistinguished birth confronts the possibility of his death," and so on. Yet if I understand this account of the poem, we would have in Crane's terms a kind of dramatic monologue appropriate to the speaker and his peculiar combination of talent, education, defects, and the like; and we would know what kind of young man he was solely from the poem; and the poem would therefore be inescapably a perfect achievement, and criticism would be forestalled at the outset. Although Crane is a distinguished eighteenth-century scholar, and one with a fairly extensive knowledge of Renaissance and earlier thought, he fails to apply his knowledge. It does not occur to Crane that medieval and Renaissance poetry is formally rational and as often as not is formally logical in the technical sense;[6] that for well-known historical reasons this structure disintegrates rapidly in the eighteenth century; and that what we see in the *Elegy* is a meditation on death and on certain aspects of life, spoken not by an hypothetical young man dramatically rendered, but by Thomas Gray and to the best of his ability—a meditation in which we can see the rational structure of the great poets far gone in decay under the influence of associationism and Shaftesburian sentimentalism.[7] If we consider the poem in this light we can criticize it; we can evaluate it with reference to other and greater works. Crane puts it beyond the reach of criticism, just as he puts it outside of history.

But in spite of his elaborate defense of a study of the forms of poetry as forms, Crane does not explore any of the forms very far. He gives us a good account of the structure of tragedy as he derives it from Aristotle, with a few variations on the Aristotelian formula. What he says appears to me to be sound, but it is extremely general, and there are many problems of which he seems to be unaware, a few of which I shall indicate later in this essay. He gives a sound but very brief account of the plot of *Macbeth* as a variation on the Aristotelian formula. He has written an excellent study of the plot of *Tom Jones,* contained in *Critics and Criticism*: a workmanlike job on a simple subject. But the essay on *Tom Jones,* the few pages on *Macbeth,* and the remarks on the *Elegy* are about the extent of his practical criticism: as a critic, he is a scholarly amateur; he knows no more about criticism than Tate, Ransom, and their agrarian friends of twenty years ago knew about farming. He exhibits no knowledge of the structure or history of lyric poetry in English, and his few remarks on the subject make one suspect that he would write badly if he tried to write of it. He seems in brief to have come to poetry through an interest in criticism, rather than to criticism through an interest in poetry.

And this is a grave weakness. The poet, as poet, tries to write as well as possible. Every moment of his poetic life is thus concerned with exact and minute literary judgment, with evaluation, and he reads other poets as he reads himself, to discover what is really sound, to discover what might be improved, and in this way to improve his own intelligence and his own composition. If he has real poetic talent, reasonable scholarship, and the power of generalization, this interest may lead to the formulation of valid critical principles, more or less general and inclusive, depending on his intellectual powers. These principles may in turn free him from the tyranny of historical fashions (for we are determined by history only to the extent that we fail to understand it), may aid him to choose sounder themes and sounder methods of structure, and by virtue of these to achieve greater precision of detail. I am aware of no theoretical reason why a man not a poet should be unable to study poetry in the same way; I merely know of no such man who has done so. The professor, the learned but non-poetic critic, usually considers the exact evaluation of detail as somehow trivial, and hence his principles are vaguely conceived and often unsound, for the proof of a structure is in the quality of the details which it produces. One cannot study one aspect of poetry and achieve any really sound judgments. And, on the other hand, too many poets are unfortunately incapable of more than limited generalizations, or, having been caught in the anti-intellectual traditions of the past two hundred and fifty years, consider such generalizations unnecessary or somehow debasing. The problem of educa-

22

tion involved in this difficulty is very great, but at least a begin ning has been made in our time, and something may come of it. If all of this seems to be complicated, I can only say that the spiritual life is more arduous than even Saint Paul suspected, and we have only two possibilities from which to choose: we may endeavor to become intelligent, or we may continue to rest on our laurels— if that is what we are resting on.

Crane believes that nearly any critical method may have its uses, but he believes that certain methods may be more useful than others for certain problems (and he hints for most problems). But how does he determine which method or methods will be most useful in a given case? By pre-critical common sense. This pre-critical common sense would seem to have the balance of power in his system; if it is so important, one might think it the part of wisdom to study it and organize it into principles, yet Crane nowhere suggests this, nor does he define its nature or indicate its extent; it is simply a vague agent, of undefined power, operative at the beginning of any critical problem which we undertake. The pre-critical common sense of Crane will certainly differ from that of many critics whose methods Crane obviously dislikes, yet Crane is committed by theory to approve of their efforts, no matter how much he may dislike them in fact. If this is not relativism in theory, and irresponsible personal dogmatism in fact, it is hard to say what it is. And Crane sees criticism rather as descriptive than as evaluative, although he admits the possibility of ultimate judgments resulting from perception or taste.

One gets the impression from Crane and from his disciple Olson that works of one genre cannot be compared with works of another, yet nowhere are we told just where the impassable lines are to be drawn. Is it impossible merely to compare a lyric, say, with a tragedy? Or does the logical lyric as practiced by Wyatt and Nashe form an inviolable genre and the associationist lyric as practiced by Collins another? But if we can profitably compare for relative evaluation *In Time of Pestilence* with the *Ode to Evening,* why cannot we compare the possibilities of the lyrical forms with those of the tragedy? Such comparisons would seem to be the purpose of the study of the forms: to find out which forms offer the finest media, both in general and for particular purposes, and perhaps to modify certain forms where it is possible by drawing upon aspects of the others. Yet this kind of criticism is possible only if we have a clear idea of the function of literature in general, so that we may evaluate the forms in the light of that final cause, and Crane will recognize no such function, and he is interested in the forms chiefly, it would seem, for the purpose of keeping them distinct from each other—except where his unexamined preference for the mimetic principle tempts him to misapply it.

From these brief remarks on the leading critics of the past half century, are we to judge that criticism and scholarship do not mix after all, or at least had better remain unmixed? The answer to this is that they *are* mixed, have always been mixed, and cannot be unmixed, and we had better hold what little we have gained and try to gain a little more. The "scientific" scholar who studies literature objectively as a record of the past is deluded. He is not studying all of the literature of the past, nor even of a single period. He devotes much more time, for example, to Milton than to Sir Richard Blackmore, and quite likely he has never read Blackmore. This fact indicates that a critical judgment has been made, either by the scholar or by his predecessors. In this case it may have been easy to make, and may have required no great talent; but every writer that the scholar studies comes to him as the result of a critical judgment, simple or multiple, and many of the problems may be more difficult, and in fact they are, and in fact many of the judgments have been wrong. Furthermore, it is hard to see how our scholar will be able to write the history of poetry, let us say, when he does not know what a poem is or how it functions: for this scholar the history of poetry will be a disjointed description of discrete phenomena, all of them seen through the haze of various misapprehensions.

III.

I will endeavor to proceed.

During the past twenty years I have neglected a good many of the topics which Professor Crane says that every critic ought to consider, but I think that I have considered more of them than has Professor Crane. I have devoted myself mainly to what I think had better be called the short poem, to what Crane calls the lyric poem, and to what I have often called loosely and unfortunately by the same name. So far as I can recollect, I have written only four essays on novelists, but if this count is correct I am three ahead of Professor Crane. I have written no essays on the drama. In the course of my discussions of the short poem, I have made a good many references to the other forms of literature, where there seem to be principles cutting across the lines of the forms. Professor Crane seems to disapprove of my having done this, but he himself has done the same thing repeatedly. He disapproves of my distinction between poetry and prose, but he offers none of his own. My distinction is this: that poetry is written in verse and prose is not. It is a workable distinction, and I have written a good many pages to clarify the rather complicated ramifications of the distinction. So far as I can discover, Professor Crane includes under the heading of poetry everything that I have included under the heading of artistic literature—that is, literature which endeavors at one and the same time to clarify a subject rationally and to move the emotions appropriately—except that Professor Crane excludes what Aristotle calls works of rhetoric. I can understand the theoretical basis for this exclusion if we confine our attention to Aristotle, but I cannot help wondering how Professor Crane would use the distinction in practice. The influence of rhetorical treatises on Medieval and Renaissance prose and poetry of all kinds is so great that one can only describe it as pervasive, and almost every university of our time offers one or more seminars on the subject.

However, I have sinned. I have not dealt at length with the differences between the literary forms, any more than has anyone else in our time. Professor Crane is right in saying that some one

25

ought to have done so. Furthermore, I will not deal at length with the various forms in the few years remaining to me, for there are still aspects of what I think the greatest of the forms which I wish to explore. But I would like to profit by Professor Crane's reproof and point out a certain number of problems which I think should be examined carefully by the next generation. After all, no single man will ever be able to finish this work, neither Professor Crane nor myself.

Let me repeat first of all the assumption on which I invariably proceed as a critic. I believe that a poem (or other work of artistic literature) is a statement in words about a human experience. I use the term *statement* in a very inclusive sense, and for lack of something better. But it seems to me obvious that *The Iliad, Macbeth,* and *To the Virgins to Make Much of Time* all deal with human experiences. In each work there is a content which is rationally apprehensible, and each work endeavors to communicate the emotion which is appropriate to the rational apprehension of the subject. The work is thus a judgment, rational and emotional, of the experience—that is a complete moral judgment in so far as the work is successful. I see no escape from these opinions, any more than I can see an escape from the opinion that poetry is written in verse and prose in prose, although I am fully aware that I am far more simple-minded than nearly all of my contemporaries. I am perhaps guilty here of an act of faith; but it seems to me of the same order as that act of faith by which I believe that I am. Without one or two fundamental acts of faith, or appeals to experience, we can scarcely begin to converse. And I do not believe that the act of faith in question is really very arbitrary. After all, what is *Macbeth* or *To the Virgins?*

If we can grant as much as this, we can proceed to certain additional admissions. We may admit, with Professor Crane, that *Macbeth* is a tragedy and *To the Virgins* is a lyric; and we may as well agree with Professor Crane about the nature of tragedy in general and of *Macbeth* in particular, but I think that we had better be careful about agreeing with Professor Crane whenever he writes of the lyric.

Our experience with the poetry already written would seem to indicate this: that we regard as greatest those works which deal with experiences which affect human life most profoundly, and this criterion is not merely one of the intensity of the experience but of the generality or inclusiveness of the implications. In making this statement, I am assuming, of course, that the works in question are sufficiently successful in execution so that execution may be more or less neglected in the comparison. Execution can never be neglected, however, in our judgment of the individual works: a work which is poorly executed is bad, no matter what the conception; a form, or a sub-form, which enforces any kind of inferior writing is an inferior form, unless it can be shown that it permits greater generalization than any form which permits better writing—and then we shall have to strike a balance between the virtues and defects of the forms.

But let me illustrate what I have just said about subject matter, with reference to two tragedies, *Macbeth* and *Phèdre*. Of the two plays, *Phèdre* is certainly the better executed; in fact, so far as execution is concerned, it comes very close to perfection, within the limits permitted by its particular form, but of this I shall say more later. As regards the subject, however, we may say this: when the play opens, Phèdre is already overpowered by a passion not merely illicit but incestuous, and this passion is not of her own choosing, but in her opinion is the result of the arbitrary malice of Venus. In her great climactic speeches, she expresses awareness of her sin, it is true, but she sees herself as helpless, and the speeches are expressions of suffering only, and almost of self-pity.

Macbeth, however, is a far more complex agent. His speech at the beginning of I-vii, in which he contemplates the murder of Duncan before committing it, shows that he has a theoretic understanding of the nature and consequences of such an act, even though he seems as yet to have no imaginative realization of them. The realization comes after the act, and becomes more intense as the play proceeds; the evidence of the realization is to be found in four or five speeches by Macbeth at important points in the action, the last and most moving being the speech beginning "Tomorrow, and tomorrow, and tomorrow" in V-vi, which follows immediately upon Macbeth's two lines of comment on his queen's death. This speech, if taken out of context, may appear to refer to the tedium of time, and I dare say appears so to many casual readers of the play. But it is far from referring merely to that. Macbeth has murdered Duncan, Banquo, and the family of Macduff; and he has murdered sleep. But he has murdered more than that, and he knows it—knows it not merely in theory, now, but in fact: he has murdered his own soul. This is the speech of a man who sees himself as a walking dead man, to whom his own life has lost all meaning. These speeches, in which the general implications of Macbeth's sin are indicated, give greater precision to our understanding of the sin and give greater scope to the play: the play is not merely an account of the tragic consequences of a particular irrational passsion, as is *Phèdre;* it is an account of the tragic consequences of irrational passion. It is thus the greater play.

IV.

With these general principles in mind, let us proceed to certain problems in the judgment of narrative, whether prose or verse. The problems of subject-matter in these forms will be common to the drama as well.

In his volume *Woe or Wonder,* a collection of essays on Shakespeare, J. V. Cunningham includes an essay entitled *The Donatan Tradition.*[8] Cunningham's prose is extremely concise, and it would be folly to try to summarize it. I shall therefore merely mention two points which Cunningham makes in this essay, and I shall indulge myself in a few meditations in connecton with these two matters, meditations of which Cunningham will doubtless disapprove.

As to the first of these, I shall quote briefly. Cunningham, in summarizing certain of the views of Donatus on tragedy, says:

> The first distinction is that the tragic characters must be great, and this means of high rank. It is the modern feeling that this is

an artificial stipulation, explicable only in the erroneous social ideas of our ancestors. But *The Death of a Salesman* is not a tragedy in the old sense, and so one might conjecture that there is something else involved: there is involved a radical difference in the nature of the tragic effect. For the field of tragedy will be the state, since men of high rank will be the rulers of the state. Tragedy will then involve not private life and private feeling—this is the province of comedy—but public life and public feeling. But public feeling is different in kind from private. A public calamity moves us in a different way than does a private one. The murder of John Doe is one thing; the assassination of Trotsky or of Admiral Darlan is another. Hence the tragic emotions in the older tradition will be predominantly communal and public, and we will find that a similar qualification is implied in the other principles of order which Donatus distinguishes.

This principle seems to me sound, and it is operative in all of the great tragedies of Shakespeare; yet it is worth noting that it is less obviously operative in *Othello* than in the others, and after *Macbeth* and *Hamlet, Othello* is probably the best of them.

The second point which I wish to repeat from Cunningham, or rather by way of Cunningham from Donatus, is this: "that the plot of tragedy is commonly historical and true, not feigned . . . it has . . . the compelling absoluteness of accomplished fact. Hence its effect will be accompanied by the recognition that things could not be otherwise, since this is how in fact they were." These are two of the characteristics which differentiate tragedy from comedy, in which "the story is always made up . . . the characters are of moderate estate, the difficulties that arise are slight, and the outcome of it all is joyful." These are essential differences, briefly, between a major and a minor form.

Of the two requirements of tragic writing just indicated, historiographers, more than any other writers of prose narrative, can perhaps most easily avail themselves. Biography, in this connection, should be regarded as a branch of historiography, for the two are frequently hard to distinguish. The historical novelist might also profit by these possibilities if he had the wit to see the advantages. Macaulay's account of Monmouth's rebellion, in Chap-

ter V of the *History of England,* is a relatively short example. Both
Monmouth and James II were mediocre men, at the most chari-
table estimate, and had either been born into a mediocre estate
he would probably at most have provided the material for comedy
and James for low comedy. But James was the king of England,
and Monmouth aspired to be king. Their actions involved the
fate of England; they were public actions, not private; and they
really happened. Macaulay's prose is in the heroic tradition, yet
is capable of irony; it is rapid, exact, flexible, and deeply moving;
the paragraphs dealing with the execution and burial of Monmouth have a grandeur almost equal to that of great Shakespearian
verse. It will be almost impossible to match this prose in the works
of the English and American novelists; Melville alone, and only at
his best, is comparable. One could cite other examples from Macaulay and from other historians, but this one example will have to
suffice. The point which I wish to make is this: that Macaulay had
a great subject and hence was able to write great prose. He had
the talent for great prose, of course, but he could not have exer-
cised it without the subject. An important part of his talent lay
in his ability to find the subject.

Let us consider the subject of *The Age of Innocence,* by Edith
Wharton. The setting is in the aristocratic society of New York,
in the 1870's, a period in which the society had lost its religious
convictions and its moral ideas but still retained its moral habits,
the habits being embodied for the most part in social forms. For
most of the members of the society these forms were merely forms,
although they were respected with a kind of frozen gentility which
had replaced the earlier religious beliefs. The two principle characters, Newland Archer and Ellen Olenska, understand both the
virtues and the superficialities of this society, and so does Mrs.
Wharton. Archer and Ellen decide not to elope, in part because
of their realization of these virtues, in part because of mere social
pressure, and to the extent that the second cause is operative the
moral strength of the book is attenuated. The book is not a tragedy in the Elizabethan sense, but neither is it a comedy, although
it contains comic materials. The central characters surrender a
private good in the interests of a public good, however frail and

far gone in decay the latter may be; in a small and gentle way they give up life to gain life. In these respects the book is serious, and the prose is adequate to the materials. But the question of whether or not Newland Archer shall elope with his wife's cousin is an extremely private and particular question. We do not have a great subject, and since Mrs. Wharton had critical tact, she did not try to write great prose: the prose is precise, perceptive, and intelligent, but it is not great. In *The Writing of Fiction* Mrs. Wharton warns the prospective fictionist of the danger inherent in subjects which are too great for his power; there is a trace of melancholy in her warning, as if she were thinking of herself. I have always had the feeling that if she had chosen to write a novel on the life of Woodrow Wilson, she would have constructed her plot from the incident of his second marriage.

Is the character of high estate essential to the serious subject, however? I suspect that the chief virtue of this kind of character lies in his power to generalize the subject, to extend its significance beyond the limits of particular experience, and although it may well be that the greatest possible generalization is impossible without this kind of character, yet this kind of character is obviously not the only means to such generalization. *Macbeth* and *Phèdre* both employ such characters, and both fulfill the traditional requirements for tragedy; yet *Macbeth,* as I have tried to show, is the more generalized of the two, and for a reason irrelevant to this one. There might well be tragic possibilities in the predicament of the German and other European professors who refused to betray the principles of scholarship at the insistence of the Nazi government; they were not of high estate in the technical sense, but they were at least in conflict with those who were, and—what might prove to be more important—they represented something greater than the State and were conscious of the fact. It is possible that the labor leaders of fifty or sixty years ago might have a measure of the same power. Frank Norris, in *The Octopus,* had characters and a situation, which, though more restricted than those of *Macbeth,* might yet have resulted in a greater novel than *The Age of Innocence* had he possessed the ability to understand them and sufficient education to write literate prose.

Such power as Hawthorne achieves in *The Scarlet Letter* is due to the fact that his characters are the allegorical embodiment of a religious view of human experience which really existed in the society which he depicts, and of course the clergy were persons of high estate in that small society. I confess that I find the allegorical significance of the book more ambiguous, now, than I found it many years ago, and the prose less admirable, but, as novels go, it is one of the most impressive, and its generalizing power is the principal reason. Much of its power, moreover, resides in undisguised analysis by the author, the kind of analysis that we might expect to find in an historian or biographer, and which modern novelists have in the main tried to avoid as somehow reprehensible.

Melville stresses the absolute power of Ahab on board the Pequod, and compares him to ancient kings, but he perhaps overdoes it, and the effectiveness of Ahab in the story has more important causes. Captain Vere, in *Billy Budd*, is a sea captain, but he is a captain of a naval vessel in a period of national emergency, and so is in a far more serious manner than Ahab a man of high estate, and the matter needs no great emphasis: the situation in which he finds himself makes him the representative and guardian of the social order, and consequently he becomes the embodiment of the critical intelligence. In *Benito Cereno* we have two sea captains in remote waters. In this book the Negroes are the embodiment of evil, evil which (by implication) is the result of injustice, and Babo is the representative Negro: Babo's head, at the end of the story, is almost the symbol of the inscrutable and incurable evil of the universe which had obsessed Melville through so many books. Cereno is the civilized mind which, failing to recognize evil in time, is broken by it and at the same time instructed. Delano is the sentimental optimist, the good-natured man, who sees all and understands nothing, and who is rescued partly by chance and partly by the sudden decision of the educated but broken Cereno. Both works employ the method of undisguised exposition and with great effect; the method is used more sparingly but more expertly in *Benito Cereno*. *Billy Budd* appears to be the unfinished draft of a great work. *Benito Cereno* is the most successfully written of Melville's works, and with *Moby Dick* is one of the greatest. It is deserving of careful study, I believe, for its methods and for the kinds of prose which it contains.

I hope that I may be forgiven if I devote a paragraph to a book by my wife, Janet Lewis, for the book has a certain interest in connection with the matters which I have been discussing. It is a novelette, entitled *The Wife of Martin Guerre*.[9] It is a historical novel: not only did the events really occur, but they constitute the materials of one of the more famous cases in the history of French law. The characters are not of high estate, absolutely considered, but in their own eyes their estate is anything but contemptible. They were wealthy peasants, of old peasant families, living in the south of France in the sixteenth century. Such peasants were proud of their families, of the antiquity of their families, and of the stability of the social order of which they were a part; and the events of the story threatened the social order with at least a measure of disruption. The peasants were Catholics, and their religious and moral ideas were definite and firmly held. The action of the story occurs as the result of an arbitrary act on the part of a young man who is the son of a tyrannical father. The young man has offended his father, leaves his young wife, goes off to the wars, and delays his return even after his father has been long dead. A wandering rogue who bears a close resemblance to Martin Guerre hears of the situation, studies the facts of the family history and organization, replaces the husband, and lives as Martin Guerre for several years, deceiving a large family and many old servants. The wife finally suspects him, and with difficulty convinces her uncle, and the uncle brings the case to trial. The impostor is convicted; there is an appeal and he is about to be acquitted, when Martin Guerre enters the court room. The impostor has behaved like a gentleman except for his initial sin, and has loved the lady and caused her to love him. He is sentenced to execution; Martin Guerre disowns his wife and leaves the court room. The story begins in error, proceeds to deception, is clarified by the person who must suffer most for the clarification, and ends in death: religion, morality, and the social order are the governing principles, and most of the later action takes place in the court room. This is, I suppose, as much a matter of public emotion as of private—nearly as much a matter of public emotion, let us say, as we have in *Othello*. In style, the book relies heavily on the techniques of expository summary and explanation employed by the historian, and part of its rapidity of movement is due to this reliance; certain important portions of the action are expanded into scenes, in the manner of the novelist, but the expansion is subdued to the effect of the whole. We have here, with the one qualification which I have mentioned, the principal elements of tragedy. It is my own opinion that the prose is adequate to the subject; but even if I should be misled by prejudice in this judgment, it seems to me certain that the book deserves study as an example of method.

In this portion of my essay I began to talk about the materials of prose narrative, but I was led almost inescapably into some discussion of the more traditional methods of narration. I would like to say something now about certain innovations in method which have been made in our century.

I agree with Professor Crane that every drama and novel should have a plot and that the plot should be well constructed; as a matter of fact an enormous number of such works do have such plots, but these virtues are often insufficient to overcome the limitations of the materials from which the plots are constructed and the limitations imposed by theories regarding the proper manner of revealing or developing plots. It is an easy matter to dissect the plot out of *Macbeth,* pronounce it good, and remark casually with Professor Crane that the virtues of character and diction depend upon the plot. Of course they do, but they might have been better and they might have been a great deal worse, and we would like to know why.

Professor Crane expresses briefly but emphatically an admiration for the plotting of Henry James. In this admiration he is one of a multitude, and I am another of the same multitude. But the materials of Henry James are very similar to the materials of Edith Wharton, and as I have pointed out in my essay on James, the author's understanding of them is even more severely limited than that of Edith Wharton through his failure to understand the social order from which his characters arose. And this is not the worst. James held, in his latter years, a theory regarding the development of his plot which had a considerable bearing on his procedure: he believed that the omniscient author, the historical explicator, should disappear, and that the reader should proceed through the novel by way of the minds of his characters. So far as James's procedure in the later novels was concerned, this meant that we should become one with Lambert Strether from beginning to end of *The Ambassadors*. We are born with Strether into Paris in Strether's fifty-fifth or fifty-sixth year, we pick up fragments of his past history as his mind happens to touch on it, we become aware fragmentarily of Paris and of people in Paris as Strether sees them or thinks of them for a few moments here and there; and little by little—in the manner of Strether—we form conclusions, which are replaced by other conclusions, and so on. The prose generated by this method is almost as impressionistic and fragmentary as possible. Even if we have read the book within a very few years we cannot pick it up and start the fifth or fifteenth or twentieth chapter and read with any comprehension. The virtues of narrative prose have been abandoned: narrative is present only in the total structure. The virtues of expository prose have been abandoned: we must construct our own exposition of the story when the story has been completed; and as I have pointed out in my essay on James, the author's intentions as to what our construction should be are anything but clear, for he seems to have become lost among his own perceptions. We have, in brief, a plot, if we can determine precisely what it is, and this is no small task; and we have a diffuse and confusing prose, of one kind only. And throughout the book we are forced to consider much more seriously than they merit the fragmentary details of sensory and emotional perception. The damage done by this procedure simply to the art of prose is enormous, and, as I have said in my essay on James, if the perfection of the art of the novel results in damage to the art of prose, then there is something wrong with the novel. Actually, I believe that the trouble is not with the novel but is rather with the particular kind of novel which James was trying to write.

Furthermore, this is no merely personal difficulty of my own. In Volume 22, Number 3, of *American Literature,* there appears a paper by Robert E. Young, entitled *An Error in the Ambassadors.* This paper demonstrates to a certainty that Chapters XXVIII and XXIX of *The Ambassadors* are printed in reverse order, and that James himself in revising the work for the New York Edition did not correct the error, although he altered many details of style within these chapters. Young gives a reasonably convincing account of the manner in which the error probably occurred; but the error could not have occurred and James could not have failed to detect it, had it not been for the peculiar diffuseness and obscurity of the prose. Young, when he wrote this paper, was a third-year undergraduate at Stanford, and the paper was written for my course in the American novelists (English 265). Young was nineteen years old. He was preparing for the study of law, and after leaving Stanford he entered a large eastern law school, and I am sure that he will be a good lawyer, and I wish him well in spite of the embarrassment which he caused me. I had not observed the blunder over a period of about fifteen years of teaching James, and my best students had not observed it. Young's paper caused quite a flurry among my graduate students at the time: they heard the theory with contempt and verified it with humility. A few months after Young's paper was published, a gentleman whose name I have forgotten replied to it in the same journal. His point was this: that the error had been corrected in an English edition of the novel which has long been out of print and which is practically unobtainable, and that for this reason Young was no scholar. This gentleman was obviously a scholar of the old school: he had got hold of a fact and was bound to make the most of it, but he didn't know what it meant. What the fact meant was this: that the person who had made the correction in the English edition had caught the error and that no one else had noticed it until Young came along—that no one, in fact, had even noticed the correction, for every edition of *The Ambassadors* now in print repeats the error.[10] Young's point was that the error should not have occurred, that, once it had occurred, it should not have been so hard to detect, and, if it was so hard to detect, that there was a flaw in the author's method. It should be remembered that James thought *The Ambassadors* his finest piece of work, as regards both construction and style.

I have used James to illustrate one way only in which a theory of construction may affect the art of prose. Of James I think that we may safely say this: that he is the greatest master in our literature of the most limited kind of narrative matter combined with the most unsound narrative technique antedating Joyce, Miss Richardson, and Mrs. Woolf; and in our time this is no small achievement, but I would hope for better. In the later Joyce, in Miss Richardson, and in Mrs. Woolf, plot, in various ways and degrees, has become less important; the particular detail and the progression from detail to detail by pure association have largely taken charge of the novel. The clear perception of the detail, a clarity of perception so acute that it seems to imply undefined significance, that is, Joyce's epiphany or Pound's image or ideogram, has become the essence of great writing. In an old essay on Joyce, Edmund Wilson writes as follows: "If Flaubert taught Maupassant to look for the definitive adjectives which would distinguish a given cab-driver from every other cab-driver at the Rouen station, so Joyce has set himself the task of finding the precise dialect which will distinguish the thoughts of a given Dubliner from those of every other Dubliner."[11] Let me say this: that my own interest in this kind of particularity is mild indeed, for the world is teeming with such particularity, and as we grow older we become less interested in details and more interested in such conclusions as can be drawn from details; and conversely our interest in details becomes more and more concentrated on those details from which conclusions may be drawn or which contain important conclusions implicit within them. I do not deny the virtues of accurate writing, but I insist that accuracy of detail should be subordinate to an important end, and in these writers, I think, the importance of the end is at a minimum.

In these three writers and in the later James we have an art which is mimetic in a particular sense: the author endeavors to imitate the processes by which he believes that people really think. It is true that much thought proceeds by way of sensory perception and association, but this is only one kind of thought, and it is thought at the most elementary level. There are other ways of thinking, as one can discover, for example, by reading Plato or Macaulay's history. But many of our novelists have decided that the thought of the conscious author is somehow unworthy of the serious author, and should be eliminated; that the fragmentary and unguided thought of the character, as he walks down the street, or sits in a bar, or dreams at night, should be imitated as closely as possible. I confess that I find such imitation dull, even when it is done by Joyce. I prefer the complete thought of the great mind, and the structure which is proper to such thought, and I cannot see that Joyce offers much in return for what he eliminates. If this is the novel, we pay too high a price for it.

I should like to mention one other technique which for a number of years in our century was widely used: the technique of narration by retrospection, or the extended flashback. Jonathan Colgate, in late middle age, stands at his study window and looks out upon the autumnal scene; the sky is overcast; the leaves fall; and he is melancholy as he considers the many frustrations of his life. His mind goes back to the beginnings and wanders toward the present, and on page 400 we finally understand all of the reasons for his depression. The state of mind appropriate to the conclusion has hung evenly over the entire narrative, in the manner of what Californians would call a high fog. The narrative proceeds largely by association: that is, the reader must piece it together from Judge Colgate's thoughts. The state of emotion is given at the beginning, and therefore is given in loose terms; it is explained more or less at the end; but there is no exact relationship from page to page between the narrative so far as developed and the emotion appropriate to this development—that is, there is no precision in the language, but there is rather a vague narrative technique combined with a vague emotionalism, and this combination breeds the cliché, the pseudo-poetic phrase, as dead water breeds mosquitoes. Ellen Glasgow employed this technique with all its consequences, to infinite tedium, and others have done the same.

I have not exhausted the methods of modern fiction in these

few paragraphs, nor have I analyzed exhaustively the methods I have mentioned: that has not been my purpose, and I will leave that work for others. I have merely tried to indicate a few of the critical problems before us, and by indicating those few to indicate the kind of critical problem that must be explored if the novel is to survive. For the fact of the matter is, as most intelligent critics and even novelists are aware, that the novel in our time is nearly dead. Unless there is a serious reconsideration of materials and methods, not merely in the interests of what may seem to the uninstructed to be novelty, but in the interests of intelligent achievement, the next generation will see the novel as dead as the drama is now. The most damnable fact about most novelists, I suppose, is their simple lack of intelligence: the fact that they seem to consider themselves professional writers and hence justified in being amateur intellectuals. They do not find it necessary, so far as one can judge, to study the other forms of literature, or even forms of the novel other than those they practice; they do not find it necessary to think like mature men and women or to study the history of thought; they do not find it necessary to master the art of prose. And these remarks are equally true, so far as my experience goes, of those novelists who write primarily for profit, and who boast of being able "to tell a good story," and of those who are fiddling with outmoded experimental procedures in the interests of originality and who are sometimes praised in the quarterlies. In fact the history of the novel is littered with the remains of genius sacrificed to ignorance and haste. I can read the later Joyce and Mrs. Woolf in small passages, for the details are often entertaining, even though their function may be trivial. But I cannot read the neat but simple Mr. Hemingway, nor the inarticulate (though doubtless profound) Mr. Faulkner, and I can see no reason why I should be asked to try. I am a student of literature, not an anthropologist, and I have better ways of spending the few years remaining to me.

V.

I would like to turn to the epic proper and the allegorical epic.

As I have said, I believe that the difference between poetry and prose is verse. There may be great poetry and great prose, but the medium imposes certain differences, in spite of the fact that Professor Crane has not noticed these. But the narrative arts have much in common which cuts across this division, and it may be worth our trouble to consider the effects of the division on the common elements.

Verse is metric or measured language. The measure controls the rhythm, and provides precision of rhythm. The resulting rhythm is more expressive of emotion than is the relatively loose rhythm of prose. That is, verse can express a stronger emotion than prose, and, within the limits proper to it, can express emotion more precisely than prose, even if the emotion is not strong. But it has a different range of emotion than that of prose: the total range of verse is higher, although the two ranges overlap perhaps half of the time. Thus there are subjects which verse can treat with greater power than prose; there are many subjects which verse can treat with greater precision than prose; but there are many subjects which prose can treat with propriety and which verse cannot treat without a somewhat embarrassing exaggeration. The problem with any particular work in hand is to decide which of the two mediums will be more effective the greater part of the time and in general: the decision may be far from an easy one, but one should never forget that the power of truly great prose is far from contemptible—the fact is, that truly great prose is great, although we have not seen much prose of this kind in the past one hundred years.

Neither *The Age of Innocence* nor *The Ambassadors* could have been written successfully in verse, for the subjects are too slight and both works are too dependent upon a great number of particulars, which, though no doubt necessary to the whole, are too trivial individually to bear the emphasis which verse would give them. Macaulay's *History of England* is one of the greatest masterpieces of English prose, but the work is history and the bulk of factual material is large: details concerning the economic and social life of England in the late seventeenth century, of parliamentary debates, of political and military maneuvering, of theological argument, of ecclesiastical rivalries, and of private scandals. If we regard historiography as a literary form, or rather as a group of literary forms, and I think we should, such details are appropriate to the medium, and we should not wish to dispense with them; furthermore, since we are gentlemen and scholars, we find these details interesting in themselves—they are a part of history. As bare facts they are far more interesting than Lambert Strether's subtle and more or less mistaken ruminations on the altered character of Chad Newsome. But they would never do in verse; they are material for prose.

Now the epic, as we know it in Homer, in *The Song of Roland,* and in *The Cid,* is among other things a kind of primitive history. It does not carry as much historical detail and explanation as do our later histories, for its readers—or listeners—did not require this and the poets had no access to such materials even if they had wanted them, but it carries a great deal of detail notwithstanding, and much of this material is only imperfectly fitted to verse. Furthermore, much of it is only imperfectly fitted to interest the civilized mind, except as the civilized mind may choose to engage in an act of historical—or perhaps we should say anthropological—imagination. There is no harm in such an act provided we know what we are doing, but if we cultivate our imagination too much and understand it too little, we may come to believe that *The Song of Roland* is as great a work as the *History of England,* if we are thinking about histories and epics, or, since it is a poem, an epic, and the national epic of France, that it is a greater work than such and such a short poem, let us say *Le Cimetière Marin;* and it is certainly far inferior to either of these.

The heroic treatment of the prize-fight, of the Cid's defrauding of the Jews, of the thick-headed hero's sulking in his tent, or of the idiocy which caused Roland to lose the rear guard, and of many comparable incidents, we could not put up with in the work of a modern, and the reason is not so simple as a mere change of taste. A change of taste has occurred, but it is a change from the

41

primitive to the civilized, from the childish to the adult, and this is true no matter what incidental virtues the primitive poets may have had nor how many of those virtues we may have lost. It would seem the part of wisdom to value such works as historical data and for such great poetry as we may find scattered through them, but not to over-rate them. For in over-rating them we do injustice to greater works and we cloud our own understanding. My ignorance of Greek prevents my forming an opinion of individual passages in Homer, though I am willing to believe that there are many which are great; but the total action and the details of the action are simply incapable of resulting in a great work. I can read Old French and Old Spanish well enough, and I have read the *Aeneid* in Latin, though I am no great Latinist. There are passages in the *Aeneid,* the *Cid,* and the *Roland* which I find very moving, but the general objections to these works are not altered by such passages. The question of whether the *Aeneid* suffers by virtue of being an imitation of primitive models, written in a sophisticated age, of whether or not there is a kind of genteel and corrosive condescension in Virgil's manner of writing, I shall have to leave to more expert Latinists than myself.

Paradise Lost differs in some ways from the poems I have mentioned, but most of the differences are superficial. Basil Willey, in his *Seventeenth Century Backgrounds,* gives an admirable account of the difficulties faced by Milton in attempting to compose such a poem at such a time, and it is clear that Willey does not believe that Milton overcame many of the difficulties, and in this I agree with him. The work, as everyone knows, contains a large amount of admirable poetry and some very great poetry, but the very conception in which it was cast makes it a failure as a whole if we apply to it the same standards that we would apply to an effort by ourselves. In *Paradise Lost* we have a more heightened emotional norm than we shall find elsewhere: the sentence, rhythm, and diction require a much greater uniformity of grandeur in the material than do any others in English poetry; and the grandeur is only now and then evident, and when it is lacking we have grandiloquence. A good many years ago I found Milton's procedure more nearly defensible than I find it now; I

42

find now that I grow extremely tired of the meaningless inflation, the tedious falsification of the materials by way of excessive emotion. Milton has one problem, for example, which involves an interesting variant on the Homeric method. In Homer the gods are more human than divine, and although we may find them primitive in conception, nevertheless they are not supposed to be much more intelligent than Achilles and they mingle in his affairs rather naturally. Milton, however, is concerned with a deity and with additional supernatural agents who are conceived in extremely intellectual terms: our conceptions of them are the result of more than two thousand years of the most profound and complex intellectual activity in the history of the human race. Milton's form is such that he must first reduce these beings to something much nearer the form of the Homeric gods than their proper forms, and must then treat his ridiculously degraded beings in heroic language. Most of the consequent blunders, I suppose, have been noted by other writers, but they are still there: the use of cannon in the angelic war, the preposterous, cloudy, and tedious, but extremely circumstantial details of the highway from Hell, and above all, perhaps, the disquisition addressed by God the Father to God the Son in Book III, as if the Son had any need of the Father's protracted and discursive reasoning. And of course there are others. Milton did not derive this kind of detail from Revelation. He derived these details from his own laborious imagination and from his laborious struggle with intractable material and an unmanageable form. It will not do to say that these details are necessary parts of a great whole, and that we should therefore accept them. They are necessary parts of the whole, it is true, but the fact of their necessity points to the fact that the whole is not great: they are the visible evidence of the flaw in the conception. And although the poem contains a good deal of great poetry, and poetry which I trust that we shall always retain and read with high regard, yet this is not enough to justify our regarding the total work as a success. It requires more than a willing suspension of disbelief to read most of Milton; it requires a willing suspension of intelligence.

There is also the allegorical poem, which arose in the Middle

Ages, and which was expanded to epical dimensions by Dante and Spenser.

The defects of the method are more easily seen in Spenser, since he is by far the less talented of the two poets. We may consider the dragon in the first canto of *The Fairy Queen*. The gentle knight encounters the dragon, and after many Spenserian stanzas he slays it. We eventually learn that the dragon represents Error. But the dragon in general and in all its details, and merely as a dragon, is a very dull affair; it is poorly described and poorly characterized. I do not, frankly, know what one might do to make a dragon more interesting, but it seems to me that unless one can do better than this one had better not use a dragon. In its capacity as Error, the dragon spews up a number of books and papers (along with other items), and of course the dragon is ugly, but little is done in this way to further our understanding of error: there is no functional relationship between the dragon, either in general or in detail, and that which it represents. The relationship is arbitrary, and we have to be told explicitly what the relationship is. In this example we are told in the text, though late in the incident; if we were not told in the text we would have to have it explained in a summary. The gentle knight himself suffers from exactly the same defects as the dragon, and to understand him and his actions we have to read him with a chart at our elbow, and even then the significance remains on the chart and is never functional in the poem. The poem has other defects: the clumsy and tyrannical stanza, the primitive and unvaried use of the iambic pentameter line, and an habitual redundancy; but at present I am concerned only with the incurable flaws in the method.

Dante is free of the incidental faults which I have just mentioned. In fact the corresponding virtues in Dante are striking. But much the same difficulties inhere in the form of *The Divine Comedy*. Too many of the allegorical spirits, demons, ascents, descents, gates, animals, and monsters have only the most arbitrary relationship to that which they represent, and it would be next to impossible to determine a good many of the relationships without help. The preposterous demons in Canto XXI of *The Inferno* represent evil in a general way, and they are described as irrational, unpredictable, and malicious, but most of the description is devoted to their physical ugliness, so that we merely get an extensive development of the obvious. The description, in fact, is little better than Spenser's description of the dragon, with these exceptions: that Dante is not hampered by Spenser's massively clumsy stanza, and he is a far more sophisticated master of the rhythm of the line, and of the relationship of syntax to rhythm, line, and stanza, with the result that his description is more compact and gives us the impression of movement rather than of lethargy. The vision of Dis in the final canto of *The Inferno* is even more grotesque than the account of the demons in XXI, and has the same defect.

I will illustrate the problem with a very brief example, an example which, though minor in itself, is characteristic of the method. Near the beginning of Canto I of *The Inferno,* Dante encounters three beasts, a panther, a lion, and a wolf, and we are informed in a footnote in Tozer's translation that these represent the vices of lust, pride, and avarice. In Tozer's translation, the panther (lust) appears as follows:

> . . . just where the steep ascent commenced, a panther appeared, supple and exceedingly nimble, which was covered with spotted fur; nay so greatly did it impede my progress that once and again I turned me to retreat.

The panther as such is charming, and he is naturally more charming in the Italian than in the prose translation. But he is a very mild embodiment of lust; in fact there is nothing in the description of the panther which relates him to lust. I am aware of the somewhat vague mythological association, but that is not sufficient: the subject here is the sin of lust, and nothing has been said about it. There is no philosophical understanding, no psychological insight. The panther could just as easily represent procrastination or absent-mindedness. The fault is the fault of the method—when Dante is not hampered by the method, as in some of his more direct accounts of human character, he often displays the virtues which he lacks here—but the method accounts for the total structure and for the greater part of the detail.

The epic and the allegory as I have described them will never, I think, be revived. It is not that we have lost the high intelligence of Dante or of Milton. I think in fact that we have lost certain important parts of it, but those are perhaps recoverable. The reason is that we have lost the literary innocence which made it possible for men of such extraordinary gifts to be satisfied with such unsatisfactory methods.

Since Milton there have been only two attempts at anything bearing any resemblance to epic by writers of real ability: *Moby Dick*, and the *Cantos* of Ezra Pound. Melville used materials, characters, and states of mind more diverse than one can find in any of these works, and although I have not devised any accurate and rapid method of measurement, I suspect that the bulk of his work exceeds the bulk of any of them, save possibly that of *The Fairy Queen*. He substituted prose for verse, and hence freed himself from the tyrannic overemphasis of materials proper only to prose. But after he had freed himself from the tyranny he often submitted to it: much of the writing is inflated even in the absence of any need for inflation. The prose often recalls, though most of the time it surpasses, the prose of the nineteenth-century translations of epic poetry; it sometimes recalls the prose of Shakespeare or even his verse; it sometimes recalls the prose of Dickens in his more ambitious passages. It is a curious medium, but it should have been flexible enough for most of the material had it been written with greater care. Though about a fourth of the book is very badly written, this proportion is not high if we compare it scrupulously with the other works which I have been discussing. The bad writing seems to be due less to the method which Melville selected than to his occasional attempts to emulate the defective aspects of the methods which he had rejected, and perhaps to mere carelessness and haste. *Moby Dick*, too, is an allegory, but it is an allegory arising from New England nominalism rather than from medieval realism. Every fact of the universe is seen as an individual creation of God, and hence ordered to his divine plan, but as a particular creation, not as a representative of any universal. Each fact thus has what Schneider calls a "numinous" quality.[12] The relationship between detail and mean-

46

ing is commonly closer, I think, than in Dante or Spenser, though it is sometimes arbitrary.

In our time we have had the *Cantos* of Ezra Pound, which may be an epic or not, according to your definition. The work has no narrative structure, such as that of *The Iliad;* it has no expository structure, such as that of *The Divine Comedy.* It thus avoids a variety of difficulties. There are a few loosely related themes running through the work, or at least there sometimes appear to be. The structure appears to be that of more or less free association, or progression through revery. Sensory perception replaces idea. Pound, early in his career, adopted the inversion derived from Locke by the associationists: since all ideas arise from sensory impressions, all ideas can be expressed in terms of sensory impressions. But of course they cannot be: when we attempt this method, what we get is sensory impressions alone, and we have no way of knowing whether we have had any ideas or not.

The details, especially in the early *Cantos,* are frequently very lovely, but since there is neither structure nor very much in the way of meaning, the details are details and nothing more, and what we have is the ghost of poetry, though I am willing to admit that it is often the ghost of great poetry. The images are for the most part derived from Pound's reading, which has been wide, and, one might add, scattered; and the references to the reading are commonly so tangential as to be difficult. A number of young scholars at the University of California and at Northwestern University are now engaged in running these references down, and the voluminous notes which they have provided for a few of the *Cantos* are very helpful; but the notes are almost as voluminous as the *Cantos* and can scarcely be held in the head—in fact, when the work is completed, it may well be impossible to hold them in the hand—so that we shall eventually have to read the *Cantos* with a guide more awkward than anything required by Spenser or Dante.

VI.

Let me return for a few moments to historiography and to prose fiction. As I have already said, one advantage enjoyed by the historiographer is this: that what he tells has the force of accomplished fact, it has really happened. But this is also a disadvantage, for the historiographer depends upon this particular power more heavily than does any other writer, and the human mind, no matter how learned and talented, is fallible, and the modern reader is sceptical. We have learned to read history with caution and to examine the methods and credentials of the historian. We ask: *did* this really happen, or did it really happen in this way? The question if pursued very far can sometimes be damaging. We discover that Parkman, who wrote in so authoritative a manner about the Indian, knew far less about the Indian than he might have known even at that early date; that he knew next to nothing about the religious mind and religious experience, in spite of the fact that such knowledge would have been relatively easy to acquire if he had had the intelligence to understand it; and we discover that in a variety of ways his mind was very limited. We can find similar defects, more or less numerous and more or less serious, in any famous historian, but in the abler men the defects do only occasional damage. Of those now read, Macaulay has been more attacked than most, but I think unjustly. His mistakes and prejudices are obvious, but they are a small part of the total work, and his mind as we see it throughout the history is learned, judicious, and perceptive. We can scarcely afford to discard a great mind in a peremptory fashion because of a handful of errors.

But after all, the historical work has the advantage of dealing with accomplished and influential facts. One may argue that an interest in such facts is not a literary interest, but I do not believe that we can make this distinction. A large part of the power of any literary work is derived from the subject, and if the subject of history has this advantage, then so much the better for history. On the other hand, the subject of history by virtue of this very quality is relatively unmalleable. The novelist, dramatist, or epic poet may shape his materials more or less to suit his needs, even if the materials are in a large part historical; and in this respect it is worth noting that the historian is no longer allowed the privilege of shaping scenes in the interests of dramatic propriety, nor of analyzing the emotions of his characters. He must confine himself to the material in his documents, and if he wishes to go beyond what is given, he must speculate honestly as a bystander. It is conceivable that the historical novelist might combine the virtues of both forms. The historical novel might achieve virtues comparable to those of the epic or virtues comparable to those of the tragic drama, depending on the form of the action. Either way, it would lack the advantages of verse, which are real; but it would also escape the disadvantages of verse in dealing with certain kinds of unavoidable material. The mathematical evaluation and comparison of mere possibilities is difficult; but the civilized mind being what it is, I think that the falsification involved in using the poetic method on the matter of prose has rendered the epic impossible and may have rendered the poetic tragedy impossible.

A particular kind of history, further, bears an important resemblance to the ancient epic, and may well be regarded as fulfilling the function of the epic for our society. Macaulay's history recounts the rise to power of a culture hero, William III, and his establishment of that form of constitutional government in England which is now regarded by most western peoples as the essentially civilized form of government. William achieved his end without the use of force, at least in England, but by political intrigue, parliamentary procedure, and the careful management of the stupidity of his adversaries and supporters about equally. Parliamentary debate replaces the battles between bronze-age warriors; and when the worst has been said of them, the wars of the mind are more interesting than pugilistic encounters, even though such wars may be too detailed and complex to admit of even the attempt to treat them in narrative verse. And much depends upon them: civilization depends upon them. And the prose may be, and in fact is, very fine.

Motley's *Rise of the Dutch Republic* was probably influenced by Macaulay, and the subject is similar: Motley deals with William the Silent, the ancestor of William III, with his defeat of the Spanish tyranny in the Netherlands and his establishment in the Netherlands of the essential ideas of constitutional government. Motley's prose is less uniformly excellent than Macaulay's, his exaggerations are more numerous and objectionable, and his intelligence is less comprehensive and profound, but the work is impressive notwithstanding.

There are various kinds of historiography, just as there are various kinds of novel or drama. Henry Adams' *Jefferson and Madison* bears no relationship to the epic form. Like any history it is narrative, but it is less a single narrative than a collection of narratives controlled by an intention which is expository, critical, and somewhat ironic. It is very great, perhaps quite as great as Macaulay's history, but it is different in form and intention from Macaulay's history.

These speculations on the forms of historiography will probably bore a good many historians, if they should chance to read this composition. Most historians are primarily research scholars, and quite rightly; and some probably know more about the art of historiography than I shall ever know, though only one or two have written anything on the subject worth reading. But I would merely like to insist on certain facts: historiography, whether good or bad, is a form of literature, and the best examples are among the greatest works in our literature; yet the great works of historiography are almost never studied as literature in our universities, and are completely neglected by our literary critics. The study of fiction, on the other hand, occupies a place in the curricula both of our universities and of our literary reviews, which is vastly disproportionate to the achievement of our fictionists. When we consider the relative importance of the materials of history and of fiction, the possibilities of the two forms, and the actual achievement of writers in both forms, these facts are shocking, for the superiority in achievement to date lies with the historiographers, and if the form of the novel has equal capacities the fact has yet to be demonstrated in practice.

50

VII

The poetic drama, as many people have said, is a kind of imitation. A human action with its accompanying speech is imitated through speech and action: if we see the play performed, we see the action and hear the speech; if we read the play, we read the speech and imagine the action. But either way the play is primarily a form of literature: that is, we reach the action by way of the speech, for even if we see the play performed before having read it, it has still been necessary for the performers to read it and thus understand it before performing, and it is the speech which gives meaning to the action when we see it performed.

I will continue to use *Macbeth* as an example. In *Macbeth*, we have not merely the imitation of an action, but we have a moral judgment of the action. The judgment occurs in several ways. It occurs explicitly in the form of the action: that is, Macbeth is destroyed as a result of his sins. It occurs explicitly in the comments of other characters upon Macbeth. It occurs explicitly, and more importantly, as I have said earlier, in Macbeth's comments upon himself. The kinds of judgment thus far indicated, however, are explicit, or denotative, judgments. We could have all of these and still have no more than a good prose synopsis of the play. That which makes it a living simulacrum and a living judgment is the emotion resulting from this rational grasp of the theme. Ideally this emotion should be appropriate to the action at any given stage, and the final emotion should be appropriate to our realization of the significance of the whole. And of course we do not have a simple relation, at any point, of rational understanding to emotion, but once the process begins we have a complex interplay of the two, each enriching the other, the two becoming inseparable in fact, even though we may separate them by analysis for theoretic discussion.

Of course all human productions are imperfect, and Shakespeare's plays, since they were obviously written in haste, contain a good many imperfections. But I am not interested, now, in flaws which may be due to carelessness; I am interested in flaws which may be unavoidable in the medium.

For example, at any given point in the action, the dramatist must make some particular character speak as he ought to speak at that particular point. But what do we mean by *ought to speak?* In real life people do not speak in blank verse; they do not even speak in the rhythmic and inspired prose of Falstaff, nor even of the porter in *Macbeth*. What becomes of the principle of imitation at this point? I believe that it is operative, but the operation is not as simple as the term might imply. The entire play deals with an intense action, and we should all, I imagine, be willing to assume that the perceptions of all the characters are somewhat sharpened and the thought of all somewhat accelerated and heightened by the situation. Furthermore this will have to be true of the main characters: first, simply in the interests of the play; second, because they are all, especially Macbeth, sufficiently intelligent so that this would be more or less true in real life. And if the action is to have this effect on the main characters, it will have to have at least something of the same effect on the lesser characters if the texture of the play is not to be deranged. If this heightening and sharpening of emotion and intelligence can be kept, as one might say, in ratio, there will be no difficulty. The porter is somewhat more metaphysical and literary than he would be in real life, but he is a porter in comparison with Macbeth, and so on. We shall have, in other words, an imitation which is not a real imitation; it will be a plausible imitation of an imitation; and in so far as it is successful it will be much more effective than a literal imitation could hope to be, for a literal imitation would give us very little intelligent comprehension of the action beyond that of the literal characters, whereas the imitation of the imitation introduces the intelligence of Shakespeare. With these ideas in mind, we may safely call this procedure imitation.

But there are still difficulties. Let us suppose that the dramatist is imitating the speech of a character of moderate intelligence in a situation of which the character does not in any serious sense understand the meaning. This presents an almost insoluble problem. If a poet is endeavoring to communicate his own best understanding of a human situation, that is one thing. If he is endeavoring to communicate approximately a plausible misunderstanding of a situation on the part of an imaginary character much less intelligent than himself, that is quite another. He can only guess at the correct measure of stupidity which may be proper to such a character in a given situation, whether the character is offered as an imitation or as a plausible imitation of an imitation; and whether he is successful or not, he will still be writing poetry which as poetry will be of an inferior kind. Exactly what is the target? It seems to me that the whole business must in the nature of the case be a rough approximation—and rough approximations are unfortunate affairs in the fine arts.

In Act II Scene 1 of *Macbeth,* for example, Macbeth leaves the stage to kill Duncan. Just before he goes out, there occurs the dagger speech. Macbeth is, at this point in the action, uneducated by his sin. He knows that he is engaged in a desperate business, and he is terrified, but he does not as yet realize the full nature of his business. His character, here, is that of a competent but rough opportunist, somewhat more intelligent than most men of his kind but far less intelligent than he is destined shortly to become. A novelist would be able to write about Macbeth and his state of mind, and would thus have an advantage over the dramatist, who must exhibit Macbeth's state of mind in words in some sense appropriate to Macbeth in that state of mind. The novelist could employ the best prose of which he might be capable; the poet cannot employ the best poetry of which he is capable, for such poetry would be out of character—such poetry has to wait until later, when Macbeth has been educated up to the point at which he can speak it plausibly. Yet this is not a minor and quiet situation, such as a novelist, or perhaps Chaucer, might exhibit in a quiet and unobtrusive style as a necessary step toward reaching more important matters. It is a major crisis in the life of Macbeth, and his feelings are terribly aroused, in spite of the fact that his understanding is imperfect. The situation calls for powerful statement; but the statement must be made by an imperfect intelligence.

What would be appropriate language for Macbeth at this point? It is hard to say. But we can examine what he says. The first seven lines of the speech are fine lines, plain in style, and definitive of his perplexity:

Is this a dagger which I see before me,
The handle toward my hand? Come, let me clutch thee.
I have thee not, and yet I see thee still.
Art thou not, fatal vision, sensible
To feeling as to sight? Or art thou but
A dagger of the mind, a false creation,
Proceeding from the heat oppressed brain?

But these lines are somewhat quiet and speculative, and Macbeth is on the brink of murder. The subsequent lines about the dagger add little to what has been said in the lines just quoted, but they come closer to "imitating" the distraught state of mind and they give the actor an opportunity to "ham" it. The imitation resides partly in the redundancy, partly in the broken rhythm, partly in the violent detail at the end, the gouts of blood. Now these lines may transform the passage into a plausible imitation of an imitation of a second-rate intelligence in a distraught condition, or it is possible that they fail to do this—I confess that I am unable to say. But they are not very good poetry.

We have here what I have described elsewhere as the fallacy of imitative form: the procedure by which the poet surrenders the form of his statement to the formlessness of his subject-matter. You may reply that imitative form as I have here described it is an essential part of the drama and is so justified. Let us rather say that it is an all but inescapable part of drama, at least as the Elizabethans conceived the drama, and stop with that. We have the same problem that we encounter in the later novels of Henry James: the literary form employed necessitates a certain amount of inferior writing. It seems to me that this is a defect of the form, and that we would do well to keep this defect clearly in mind when we are evaluating drama in general or any particular drama. If there is another literary form without that defect or comparable defects, then that form, within the limits of whatever it can accomplish, will be more satisfactory than the drama. Our next question would be to determine whether the more nearly perfect form is or is not more limited in its scope. We might be willing to put up with a certain amount of imperfection for a greater whole.

But I must return for a moment to the interrupted speech. About half way through the speech the dagger is abandoned and the theme of midnight horror is taken up:

> Nature seems dead, and wicked dreams abuse
> The curtained sleep; witchcraft celebrates
> Pale Hecate's offerings, and withered murder,
> Alarumed by his sentinel, the wolf,
> Whose howl's his watch, thus with his stealthy pace,
> With Tarquin's ravishing strides, toward his design
> Moves like a ghost.

It seems unlikely that Macbeth in real life would have spoken anything so elaborate, but had he done so it would doubtless have been violent; and it would certainly have been composed of stereotypes, because at this stage of his development he had only a stereotyped understanding of what he was doing: he would probably have found this speech satisfactory in a play. But the fact remains that it is a more or less standard huffing speech, containing something of Marlowe and a little of Pistol; and although it contains a little of Shakespeare in addition, it is far below the great speeches in the play. When I say *far below* I do not mean, necessarily, with respect to the subject, but I mean with respect to the way in which the subject is expressed. Is it appropriate? What would be appropriate? It is hard to say. But once again, it is not very good poetry.

Let me hasten to say that I regard *Macbeth* as the greatest play with which I am acquainted and a great work of literature. I have chosen it for this reason, for even in *Macbeth* the difficulties of the form appear. These difficulties are not exceptional, but are common. I could illustrate them further in *Macbeth,* and with progressively greater ease and in greater bulk in the lesser tragedies. And after the half dozen best tragedies, if we remain in Shakespeare, and almost everywhere after we have left Shakespeare, the defective passages of this kind make up the greater part of the whole of every tragedy we may read.

Racine avoids some of this trouble, but I doubt that the result is more satisfactory. His characters, no matter what nation or time they belong to nominally, are characters of the court of Louis XIV. They are highly civilized ladies and gentlemen, who in serious situations behave with a kind of uniform propriety. They are stylized; except in the most subtle ways or at the most extraordinary moments, their personal differences hardly appear. Most of the speeches are plain exposition or argument. The characters, since they are civilized and are all of the same social habit, can speak in a manner which is appropriate at once to the matter under discussion and to their own natures; but their own natures are all very much alike, at least so far as they appear in habits of speech. The writing is effective in developing, or perhaps one might better say in exposing, the extremely skillful dramatic structure, but otherwise it is uninteresting except at certain moments of dramatic crisis, moments at which occur the long set speeches, both expository and impassioned, the *tirades,* which are so characteristic of French tragedy. *Phèdre,* in subject and in structure, is probably no more remarkable than any of four or five other plays by Racine; but it is the most famous, and probably the greatest, and the reason, I believe, is to be found in the great *tirades*: the most famous of these occur at the end of Scene iii of Act I and in Scene vi of Act IV. The plays are elaborate and precise mechanisms for exhibiting dramatic action which rises at certain moments to great poetry; but there is a great deal of mechanism in proportion to the great poetry—the great poetry is dependent on an enormous proportion of merely particular information.

I think that some of the flaws inherent in poetic drama show up more clearly in comedy, for example, in *Volpone.* The play opens with Volpone's address to his gold. The passage is remarkable. If we consider it merely as a poem, and without reference to the play, it is an exercise in intense and ingenious rhetoric which overemphasizes the importance of its subject. But this overemphasis is precisely the point of the passage with reference to the play, for Volpone is a miser; in fact Volpone is not even a character in the ordinary sense, but is an embodied abstraction, the ideal of the miser incarnate. We do not have the same problem here that we have in the dagger speech in *Macbeth,* for Macbeth is the imitation of a man, and hence Shakespeare had a good deal to distract and confuse him. But Volpone is an embodied abstraction, and Jonson can deal with him on purely theoretic grounds and do it correctly. Volpone, for example, addresses his gold with a passion which is almost sexual; and when he falls in love with Celia he sees her in terms of gold and jewels.

But Volpone is trivial in spite of his intensity. He represents a limited and contemptible passion. Hence, in the opening speech and in others, Jonson is bringing his brilliant poetic talent to bear upon a subject of minimal importance. Jonson, of course, knew this: this is comedy, and comedy is a minor form; furthermore, not only did Jonson know this, but his whole intention in the play is to demonstrate this, to convince us of this for our own improvement. But the fact remains that in spite of brilliant writing we have an extended elaboration of trivial material, and eventually it becomes tedious. Jonson, like Shakespeare, is handicapped by the mimetic principle: Dryden was able to depict Shadwell in Dryden's language and to relate him directly to Dryden's principles; Jonson was forced to depict Volpone in Volpone's language and with relation to Volpone's principles. Jonson did a remarkably brilliant piece of work, if one considers the limitations of his medium, but Dryden did a better—it would not be hard to devise a very good argument to the effect that Dryden's Shadwell, as we get him in *MacFlecknoe* and in the portrait of Og in the second part of *Absalom and Achitophel,* is the greatest comic figure in our literature. Yet Jonson was a far greater poet than Dryden; the evidence lies elsewhere.

The intensity, however, is the essence of Volpone and of the other characters equally, with the exception, perhaps, of Celia and Bonario, who are naive human beings astray among walking psychoses. The intensity, wherever it appears, is the result, not merely of Jonson's intense diction, but even more of Jonson's peculiarly sharp syntax and nervous rhythm. The reader who is trained in poetry can observe all this. The actor, however, who in our time is trained to consider poetry as an obstacle, is likely to destroy entirely this peculiar virtue of the play. And even the best actor might have trouble in rendering this virtue in its entirety, for the difficulties of projecting the voice to a large audience, while still exhibiting the subtleties of the text, and of coördinating the movements of the voice with the slow and clumsy movements of the human body, would seem to render the task impossible.

If we are to read the play instead of seeing it, there is a great deal that makes very dull reading indeed: most of the material involving the Would-Be's and most of that involving Volpone's household entertainers, and perhaps more. Some of this might be saved by skillful acting—I am insufficiently expert in matters of this kind to offer an opinion. But this would seem certain: that if the play is read, much of it is dull; that if the play is acted, a good deal of the rest is certain to be badly damaged. That is, we have a bastard form, which is neither this nor that.

The same difficulty is present in *Macbeth*, though it is far less obvious there, for the subject is serious and hence most of the minor passages are more serious than almost anything in *Volpone*. More would probably survive from *Macbeth* than from *Volpone* in the average performance, for more is present in the text; but the proportion of loss might be as great or even greater. *Macbeth* as a whole certainly bears reading better than *Volpone*. But these remarks merely indicate that *Macbeth* is the greater composition; they are not intended to obscure the flaws inherent in the dramatic form. The play in prose—let us say by Etherege, or Congreve, or Shaw—would seem to offer fewer obstacles as regards performance, for the text is closer to normal speech and demands less of the performers. But such a play offers less to the reader, for it enjoys the advantages neither of poetic style on the one hand, nor of the prose analysis of the novel on the other; it comes closer to being a mere scenario, dependent for its success upon the mechanical aids of the theater.

VIII.

My argument would seem to show that poetic composition of any kind may be more brilliant than prose from time to time, but that it is inherently defective, and will damage the total effect of any work in which it is used. Is this really true, or is there a form of literature which is essentially poetic, in which the most powerful and the most sensitive mode of writing can be used efficiently throughout? I believe that there is such a form: the short poem, or, as it is commonly, loosely, and unfortunately called, the lyric poem.

The history of this poetry follows much the same pattern throughout western Europe, although the dates of certain phenomena vary from country to country, and certain phenomena are in some countries minimized or emphasized for local reasons. The short poem reached its highest structural perfection in English in the late sixteenth century and during the first half or so of the seventeenth. The structural principle was inherited from the Middle Ages: it was that of logic. Sometimes the rigorous forms of logic are concealed or dropped, and we merely have rational discourse, but less often than one might suspect. The principle is sometimes perverted in the interests of mere cleverness, as in some of the sonnets of Sidney, but the principle is still demonstrably active. I am quite aware that simile and metaphor, involving sensory perception, are often used in these poems, although very often they are not, and that there are sometimes elements in such poems to which one might refer figuratively as narrative or dramatic; but all of these are subordinate to the formal principle which I have just named, as rational discourse in the drama is subordinate to the dramatic principle.

In the latter seventeenth century the form of the short poem began to decay, under influences which were later to be summarized as Shaftesburian deism on the one hand and associationism on the other. The beginnings of the decay can be seen in the shorter poems of Milton, and in fact in many passages in the long works; the decay progressed rapidly throughout the eighteenth century; it remained as a kind of endemic confusion throughout the nineteenth century, although by the end of the century there were signs of recovery in Bridges and Hardy. In the twentieth century, poetry seems to have moved in two different and clearly defined directions: the decay of form has progressed rapidly in men such

59

as Pound and Eliot; on the other hand there is a recovery of form in the best work of others, for examples, Robinson, Stevens, Tate, Louise Bogan, Cunningham, Kunitz, and Bowers.[13] In the nineteenth century in France Baudelaire and sometimes Leconte de Lisle are a part of this movement toward recovery, and the greatest representative of the movement is a Frenchman of the twentieth century, Paul Valéry.

The short poem, then, is not essentially imitative or narrative, but expository.[14] It may deal with trivial subjects, and most often does; but those subjects are no more trivial than the subjects of most of our novels, and the treatment can be appropriately brief and may be extremely charming. But the short poem is not confined to trivial subjects, as one may observe by reading Jonson's *A Farewell to the World* or Baudelaire's *Le Jeu*. The shortness of the short poem is due, not to triviality of subject, but rather to the formal principle involved. The other forms which I have been discussing are constructed from the depiction, interrelation, and explanation of many details: that is, they are all, in Crane's sense, imitations of action. The short poem is not an imitation of action.

From the time of Aristotle to the present it has been assumed rather carelessly that the depiction of action is the greatest achievement of the literary artist, and that those forms which do not depict action or which depict it incompletely are minor forms. But I have never seen a defense of this notion that extended beyond a few sentences or that could bear serious inspection. It is true that human life is composed of action of one kind or another, and that action has consequences, and so on. But the depiction of action per se would not be helpful: it would be meaningless. *Macbeth* is a great play not because it depicts action, but because the action is so ordered and the comments upon the action are such that we can judge the action fully and intelligently. The greatest passages in the play are a part of the action, it is true, but their greatness lies in the fact that they comment upon the action, drawing it together and giving it meaning. Without such passages the play would be inferior to *The Spanish Tragedy;* it would be less than melodrama.

The important thing is not action in itself, but the understanding of action. And I respectfully submit that such understanding can be communicated in general terms, and without the details of a particular story. Life is full of action; we can see it about us and read of it in the newspapers; we are too much involved in it ourselves. It is the raw material of generalization. But I see no reason why the poet should not be as free to generalize directly from what he has seen as the theologian or philosopher. Among the practitioners of the various disciplines of abstract thought there has long been a tendency to regard the mimetic arts with contempt, and although I think that this contempt is due in part to insensitivity and to defects of theory, I think that it may be due also to a perfectly understandable boredom with the infinite repetition of the obvious. There comes a time in the lives of some men when the spectacle is no longer informative but the theory is packed with meaning. The master of the short poem is the poet who deals primarily with the understanding of action, and since his medium is verse he can render as fully as possible the total understanding, not merely the rational but the emotional as well. Since everything that he has to say is important, not merely in relation to the whole poem but in itself, his materials will justify the use of verse throughout his poem.

For the past two hundred and fifty years it has been common to assume that abstract language is dead language, that poetry must depict particular actions, or if it be "lyric" that it must be revery over remembered sensory impressions, according to the formula of the associationists. But these assumptions are false. They are our heritage of confusion from Hobbes and Locke, by way of Addison, Hartley, and Alison—and more recently by way of Ezra Pound. A race that has lost the capacity to handle abstractions with discretion and dignity may do well to confine itself to sensory impression, but our ancestors were more fortunate, and we ought to labor to regain what we have lost. The language of metaphysics from Plato onward is a concentration of the theoretical understanding of human experience; and that language as it was refined by the great theologians is even more obviously so. The writings of Aquinas have latent in them the most profound and intense experiences of our race. It is the command of scholastic thought, the

61

realization in terms of experience and feeling of the meaning of scholastic language, that gives Shakespeare his peculiar power among dramatists, and Fulke Greville his peculiar power among the English masters of the short poem. I do not mean that other writers of the period were ignorant of these matters, for they were not, and so far as the short poem is concerned there were a good many great poets, four or five of whom wrote one or more poems apiece as great as any by Greville; but the command in these two men is not merely knowledge, it is command, and it gives to three or four tragedies by Shakespeare, and to fifteen or twenty poems by Greville, a concentration of meaning, a kind of sombre power, which one will scarcely find matched elsewhere at such great length in the respective forms.

It would be sufficient gratification for me, if I could write one or two poems as great as George Herbert's *Church Monuments* or Ben Jonson's *To Heaven,* as Wallace Stevens' *The Course of a Particular*[15] or J. V. Cunningham's *The Phoenix.* These poems are all on great subjects; the writing of all is as nearly perfect as writing will ever be. They are profound and civilized in all their details; one can turn to them endlessly; they remain in the mind; they alter the mind; they become a part of one's life. But the human spirit is restless, and one is tempted to consider the ideal possibility of still greater achievement in the finest of the literary forms.

Baudelaire, for example, planned *Les Fleurs du Mal* not as a mere collection, but as a book. But one does not plan such a book as one might plan a novel: the planning begins with the planning of one's life. Such a book should, in theory, explore as wide a range of experience as possible, and with as much understanding as possible. This calls for a knowledge of the history of literature and ideas, for a knowledge of one's own period, for a grasp of the relationship between ideas and action on the one hand and ideas and style on the other. It calls for a command of the minutiae of style. And it calls for both patience and genius. The actual writing of such a book will be important, but most of the work will be in the preparation. Baudelaire obviously did not meet all the requirements which I have enumerated, but he met some of them fully, and he had at least an inkling of the rest. His book was marred in many ways by his personal eccentricities and by his personal history. The source of his greatest strength was likewise the source of his greatest weakness: his Romantic background. He did not entirely cure himself of his own Romanticism, and as a result some of his poems are very bad and a good many are marred. But his knowledge of the essential viciousness of Romanticism, combined with whatever he retained from his Catholic training, seems to have given him the extraordinary insight into tragic weakness which is the matter of his great poems. Whatever the flaws of the book as a whole, it is a great book; and it contains some of the greatest poems ever written. Furthermore the book points perhaps more clearly than any other to what such a book should be. And I hope that I may be forgiven if I add—for after all I, too, am a professor of a sort—that it points to one of the things that might be accomplished by a civilized department of literature, for the training necessary to the production of the ideal book of this kind will have to begin early. And the early training would not be wasted even if the book were not produced.

And then there is Paul Valéry. Valéry definitely did not produce the great book. Most of his work—and the bulk is small— deals with minor themes, and though it is sensitive and interesting, it often lacks clarity both of outline and of detail. His prose is fragmentary and somewhat affected, and it seems to me that he plays somewhat irresponsibly with somewhat childish ideas, at any rate when he is writing of poetry. But in the course of his lesser work he accumulated ideas about certain related themes, and these were organized mainly in two poems, *Le Cimetière Marin* and *Ebauche d'un Serpent*, which so far as my knowledge and judgment will guide me are the two greatest short poems ever written. The first of these is the simpler to grasp, and hence is the better known. The second is the greater. I will try to give an account of it.

As short poems go, it is a trifle long: it contains thirty-one stanzas, each stanza containing ten octosyllabic lines. The rime-scheme varies at will. It is a monologue spoken by the Serpent in the Garden of Eden, and deals with the Serpent's relationship to God, with the temptation of Eve, and with the nature of evil. The poem employs the Judaeo-Christian myth and depends upon the Christian concept of evil as privation; but it is neither Jewish nor Christian in the full development of its thought. The general theme is approximately this: God, or perfect being, had existed in a state of immobile perfection; the created universe is a flaw in this perfection—God, tired of the pure spectacle of himself, destroyed his own perfection, dissipated his principle into consequences, his unity into stars. Heaven is his error, Time is his ruin, and with them the gaping and animal abyss. The Serpent was the first and greatest creature, who now illuminates the diminution of God with all the fires of the Seducer. The Serpent had loved God to the point of complete loss of self; but he now hates him equally, for he realizes that by virtue of being a creature he is imperfect, deprived of the knowledge which as an intellectual creature he infinitely desires, and so damned. God was aware of his error when he created man, and his breath upon the clay was a sigh of despair. The Serpent hates men created in the image of God, just as he hates God, who creates so many imperfect prodigies; the Serpent is the one who modifies and retouches, and who will, in other words, seduce mankind from its simple and animal felicity to the same passion for unobtainable knowledge which is the source of his own agony. It is notable that Adam does not appear in the poem, except as his existence is implied occasionally by plural forms. The Serpent is the conscious and energetic intelligence, the intelligence of male genius, the mind of man. Eve is the common human intelligence, female, her soul as yet stupid at the threshold of the flesh. Eve is being seduced into a desire for infinite knowledge, but the psychological pattern is that of a sexual seduction; the psychological details, however, are not merely psychological but are metaphysical as well. Eve falls, and the Serpent is saddened. The Tree of Knowledge is shaken, and then the Serpent addresses the Tree in the final stanzas, stanzas in which he turns away from the somewhat pathetic and trivial sin of seducing Eve to his original desire for unobtainable knowledge. He is so created that he desires infinite knowledge, and he is so created that he cannot have it. The desire is his nature, his greatness, his sin, and his torture, and it is inescapable. The Tree grows infinitely toward infinity; the Serpent (this old expert at chess) cradles himself in the branches, so that the fruit trembles and falls: the fruit of death, despair, and disorder. The Serpent offers to the glory of God the triumph of his own sadness; and the thirst which made the tree gigantic exalts even to Being (or God) the strange Omnipotence of Nothingness (the Serpent). The theme is the most inclusive of tragic themes: one might describe it as the theme of tragedy.

Some of Valéry's French admirers have had a good deal to say about Valéry's use of sibilants, the hissing sounds, in obtaining his effects. The sibilants are, of course, there, although one can overemphasize this sort of thing, for French, like English, is full of sibilants. However, it is true that the poem is onomatopoetic: it is literally constructed in terms of the movement and sounds of the Serpent. At certain points the Serpent explicitly refers to the similarity between the movements of his thought and the movements of his body, as in the fifth stanza, which is part of the address to the sun. The italics are mine:

> Verse-moi ta brute chaleur,
> Où vient ma paresse glacée
> *Rêvasser de quelque malheur*
> *Selon ma nature enlacée . . .*
> Ce lieu charmant qui vit la chair
> Choir et se joindre m'est très cher!
> Ma fureur, ici, se fait mûre;
> Je la conseille et la recuis,
> *Je m' écoute, et dans mes circuits,*
> *Ma méditation murmure. . . .*

In the twenty-fourth stanza, we are at the crisis of the seduction. The Tree of Knowledge is caressing one of Eve's breasts with its shadow; the other breast shines like a pistil. Eve's breath now sings to the Serpent, asking him to tempt her further: "*Siffle, Siffle!* me chantait-il!" And then:

> Et je sentais frémir le nombre,
> Tout le long de mon fouet subtil,

> De ces replis dont je m'encombre:
> Ils roulaient depuis le béryl
> De ma crête, jusqu' au péril!

The excitement of the Serpent vibrates the length of his body, from his head to his tail, and beyond, into a kind of purely spiritual electricity. This is one of the few stanzas which end in a couplet, and one of the advantages of the varying rime scheme can be observed here: the couplet accelerates the movement and intensifies the excitement.

There are other explicit statements of this relationship, but these two will have to serve. The structure of the poem is that of a closely controlled development by association. The controlling theme is that of the metaphysical concept of the creation which I have mentioned and the necessary effect of such a creation upon the intellectual creature. The metaphysical concept is defined at length in several passages, as are the Serpent's love and hatred for God and for Eve. There is nothing resembling the free association of Pound's *Cantos;* but we have rather an imitation of the psychological movement of a great mind back and forth among closely related topics, the shifts occurring as the passion aroused by one topic suggests an aspect of another topic. Furthermore this mind is also the mind of Valéry, for the Serpent's metaphysics are Valéry's metaphysics, and Valéry sees the tragedy as inevitable.[16] There is no surrender of form, therefore, to a dramatic subject inferior to the author: Valéry is able to write at his best at all times. He is able, in these ways, to borrow something from the dramatic method and something from the associationists, without sacrificing the essential form of the short poem, that of exposition, or its essential virtue, the most intelligent writing possible, not merely as regards the total structure, but in every detail. And the progression of the poem from topic to topic and back again suggests the movement of the Serpent: it is sometimes slow and meditative, sometimes slow and impassioned, sometimes rapid and impassioned, but the timing is beautiful: the movement of the mind is always visible and audible. The long stanza, with its short lines and changing rime scheme, is an instrument beautifully chosen for this end.

I would like to say something about the peculiar quality of the imagery, which I think is essentially new, although one can find it elsewhere in our century, for example in certain passages and short poems by Wallace Stevens. At the beginning of the eighteenth century the third Earl of Shaftesbury summarized the anti-intellectual notions which had been developing in the seventeenth century and organized them into a loose system. About twenty years later Pope summarized these and a few additional concepts in his *Essay on Man*. Pope was able to tell us that instinct must go right, while reason may go wrong, and to add that "Equal is common sense and common ease." By the time of Pope the ideas were generally accepted by men of letters, and the elaborate ethical system by which earlier poets had understood human nature had been repudiated. The abstract statement of the great poets of the Renaissance degenerated into the eighteenth century cliché, which, however, still has the virtue of a kind of vague formality; the eighteenth century cliché, in turn, was replaced in the nineteenth century by mawkish and amateur moralizing wherever abstract statement was attempted. While the quality of abstract statement was deteriorating, such statement was being replaced rapidly by descriptive detail. Hobbes and Locke had taught that ideas arise from sensory impressions: Addison taught that the business of the poet was description, largely in visual terms, and this doctrine was elaborated by later writers. In the descriptive poems of Thomson, the Wartons, and others, there is the obvious assumption that the enthusiastic description of the merely visible is in some obscure way a pious act. If one will compare the selections in the *Oxford Book of 17th Century Verse* with those in the *Oxford Book of 18th Century Verse,* one will scarcely fail to be astonished not merely by the deterioration of poetic style but by the completeness of the deterioration and by the rapidity with which it occurred. The condition of poetry did not alter noticeably in the nineteenth century. Here and there, as in a few passages in Wordsworth or in the *Ode to Autumn,* the description is admirable, and there are a few solid poems: Wordsworth's *Ode to Duty,* Browning's *Serenade at the Villa,* Christina Rossetti's *A Pause of Thought,* and perhaps a few others; but there is not much

67

intelligence until one gets down to Bridges and Hardy. The situation in French is roughly comparable, although French poetry shows much more intelligence than does English from the time of Baudelaire and Leconte de Lisle onward.

From time to time in this period of depression a curious phenomenon occurs. *The Tiger,* by Blake, is a good example of it. The Tiger is the God of this Universe, the Spirit of Evil. In the poem he is a symbol of evil. But the poem contains no definition of evil, either implicit or explicit, and this is fortunate, for Blake regarded the rational mind as the source of all evil. The poem gives us not merely a tiger, but a kind of superlative tiger. So far as evil is concerned one can deduce the notion only from the feeling of the poem, from the obscure and bardic exaltation and from the violence of the often brilliant description. In other words, we get an intense description of a tiger, and a vague feeling of evil; or to put it another way, the matter described is described with so much genius and with a tone of such high conviction, that it seems to mean more than it does, and succeeds in duping not merely the reader but the writer. Needless to say, this was not the procedure of Donne and Jonson. But it was the procedure of Verlaine, a sensitive and sentimental poet of no great force, and of Rimbaud and Mallarmé, both of them far more talented poets than Blake. We can see it in our own time and language in Hart Crane, a poet indirectly influenced by these Frenchmen and directly by Blake. And these three Frenchmen, Mallarmé in particular, were Valéry's immediate and respected predecessors.

The concentration on the sensory perception resulted in a great deal of turgid and repetitious writing; but it also, especially as practiced by such masters of self-hypnosis and of the skills of undirected connotation as those I have mentioned, resulted in an extraordinary sensitivity to sensory perception and in an extraordinary sophistication in its expression and management. Of this sensitivity and sophistication, Valéry was the inheritor, and he added to what was left him by his ancestors, but he was not satisfied with it in a pure state. In Valéry we have this heightened sensory awareness, and we have the tone which convinces us that the details have meaning; but we also have the meaning, and the meaning is of quite as fine a quality as the rest. The image is different in kind, however, from almost anything one will find in the Renaissance, whether French or English. In Ben Jonson, for example, the language is almost purely abstract; in George Herbert and many others sensory details are named or implied, but not to be seen or heard; where we get a sensory image which is intended to affect our senses as well as our intellects, as in *The Lamp*, by Vaughan, or as in Donne's *Valediction of His name in a Window*, we ordinarily get an explicit and fully developed simile or metaphor. But in Valéry we get something else, at least as a rule: we get the sharp sensory detail contained in a poem or passage of such a nature that the detail is charged with meaning without our being told of the meaning explicitly, or is described in language indicating such meaning indirectly but clearly. The method is every bit as fine as that of the Renaissance poets, so long as the poet practicing the method has the necessary qualifications. I will give one example of this kind of imagery from the first stanza of *Le Cimetière Marin*:

> Midi le juste y compose de feux
> La mer, la mer, toujours recommencée. . . .

> Noon the precise composes there of fires
> The sea, the sea, forever rebegun. . .

Noon, or the sun at high noon, appears to be creating the sea from moment to moment, because we perceive the sea by way of the sunlight, and the moving sea is alive with the many diamonds of imperceptible foam which are mentioned a few lines later. "Forever rebegun": the sea appears to be starting over from moment to moment, because it is forever sinking and rising, simultaneously sinking and rising; but the phrase, if I remember rightly had been used previously by Bergson (and the idea, of course, by Heraclitus) to describe the total universe, and even without this clue we should presently be aware that more is being given us than the visual image. The sun is the image of the First Cause who creates the physical universe perpetually, from moment to moment, and the sea, though not the sole representative of the created universe

69

in this poem, is the primary representative. One may find something here and there in the Renaissance which resembles this method, but I do not think that the resemblance will often be very clear.

In *Ebauche d'un Serpent* we have three dominant images: the Serpent, Eve, and the Tree of Knowledge; and we have an additional concept, which dominates all of them, that of the Creator. Every particular image is informed with meaning because of its relationship with one or more of these. And since the Creator is of necessity a metaphysical concept, a great deal of the language is not immediately involved in sensory perception—much more of the language than one may suspect on a casual reading; but the purely metaphysical language and the language of sensory perception reflect upon each other, inform each other, so that we have the impression of a more or less continuous texture. The physical details live in this texture with a kind of electrical energy. In the detail, just as in the structure, Valéry has recovered what was usable in the innovations of the decadence, and has incorporated this with what was best in the traditional method.

I wish now to give a brief outline of the development of the poem, and if the reader should have a copy of the poem at hand, I would be grateful if he would open his book and follow me—follow me, bearing in mind what I have said about the general theme, the manner of developing the theme, and the qualities of the language. My account of the development of the poem will not be complete: I will merely attempt to indicate the method, and will leave the examination of all the details to the reader.

In the first stanza, the Serpent describes himself as a sophisticated and malicious animal. The second stanza continues this theme, but in connection with it introduces the Serpent's love of sunlight and his threat to the human race. The two new elements introduce the third stanza by way of association; for the sun warms the serpent, as animal, to intense activity, and the sun is the most magnificent of his accomplices, is the one who prevents humans from knowing that the universe is merely a flaw in the perfection of Non-being; and these considerations remind the Serpent that this was the place where he enjoyed the spectacle of the Fall of Man.

His memory of the Fall of Man brings the Creator to mind—"O Vanité! Cause Première!"—and we have the definition of the error of creation in stanzas six and seven. Stanza eight is the climax of this passage, and tells us of the Serpent's love and hatred of the Creator, and of the despair of the Creator when he breathed life into man, a despair which is shared by the Serpent throughout the poem:

> Objet radieux de ma haine,
> Vous que j'aimais éperdument,
> Vous qui dûtes de la géhenne
> Donner l'empire à cet amant,
> Regardez-vous dans ma ténèbre!
> Devant votre image funèbre,
> Orgueil de mon sombre miroir,
> Si profond fut votre malaise
> Que votre souffle sur la glaise
> Fut un soupir de désespoir!

Stanza nine and the first four lines of ten deal with the Serpent's contempt for the Creator's new creatures, and in fact his hatred for them:

> A la ressemblance exécrée,
> Vous fûtes faits, et je vous hais!
> Comme je hais le nom qui crée
> Tant de prodiges imparfaits!

The remainder of ten, and all of eleven and twelve are devoted to the Serpent's powers of temptation:

> Je suis Celui qui modifie,
> Je retouche au coeur qui s'y fie . . .

and these lines display extraordinary understanding of human nature.

In stanza thirteen, Eve is introduced in person, and the recollection of the temptation begins. The temptation occupies fourteen stanzas, and I can give only a short account of it. The Serpent

71

has already expressed his hatred of the new creatures, and the hatred is real; but he is in love with Eve:

> Ève, jadis, je la surpris,
> Parmi ses premières pensées. . . .
>
> Les plus purs s'y penchent les pires,
> Les plus durs sont les plus meurtris. . . .
> Jusques à moi, tu m'attendris,
> De qui relèvent les vampires!

And yet the love and hatred remain mixed and result in an accurate and cynical understanding of Eve's character:

> La superbe simplicité
> Demande d'immenses égards!
> Sa transparence de regards,
> Sottise, orgueil, félicité,
> Gardent bien la belle cité!
> Et par ce plus rare des arts,
> Soit le coeur pur sollicité;
> C'est là mon fort, c'est là mon fin,
> A moi les moyens de ma fin!

The understanding of Eve's character leads to a subtle and successful seduction, the details of which I must leave to the reader. The seduction leads to the melancholy indifference of the Serpent:

> O follement que je m'offrais
> Cette infertile jouissance:
> Voir le long pur d'un dos si frais
> Frémir la désobéissance! . . .

And at the same time the Tree of Knowledge is shaken, as it frees its essence of wisdom and of illusions.

Then follows the great address to the Tree of Knowledge, a single sentence of twenty-four lines, in which we see the Tree, as tree, growing downward and upward forever, and the Serpent, "Reptile aux extases d'oiseau," cradled in its branches:

> Berceau du reptile rêveur
> Qui jeta l'Ève en rêveries. . . .

The triumph over Eve is regarded from a slightly melancholy but essentially indifferent distance, but even in the concluding lines the Serpent sees himself as the adversary—"ce vieil amateur d'échecs"—and his eyes cause the treasures of the Tree to tremble, and from the treasures there fall the fruits of death, despair, and disorder; and we see the Serpent finally in his essential predicament:

> Beau serpent, bercé dans le bleu,
> Je siffle, avec délicatesse,
> Offrant à la gloire de Dieu
> Le triomphe de ma tristesse . . .

And in the last three lines he addresses the Tree:

> Cette soif qui te fit géant,
> Jusqu'a l'Être exalte l'étrange
> Toute-Puissance du Néant!

The primary theme is the descent from perfection to imperfection in the act of creation, and the plight of the intellectual creature whose desire is for the infinite perfection of which he is deprived and who realizes that his nature is evil by virtue of the privation; this provides the expository form of the whole poem. Subsidiary to this is the exhibition of the character of the creature in question, the Serpent, both in his philosophical meditations and in his account of the seduction of Eve. Incidental to all this is the action of the seduction and the characterization of Eve. The matter of the poem is important at every point; there is nothing trivial, either because of inherent foolishness or because of its particularity; there is nothing, therefore, which is embarrassing to the poet as poet. The poem is great in its conception, complex but clear in the organization of the conception, and all but miraculously successful in the realization of every detail. No suspension of intelligence is required of us; in fact we shall have to keep our intelligence wholly alert if we are to follow the poem. No question of belief or disbelief in a myth is involved, for the myth is not offered as a myth—it is offered as a figure of speech. I do not wish to give the impression that I am trying to startle my readers for my own entertainment, but I have studied this poem for a good many years, and in my opinion it is the greatest poem which I have ever read, regardless of kind.

IX.

This essay has been merely a rapid outline, and I have allowed myself space for only a minimum of analysis and illustration. The opinions which I have offered are the result of a good many years of reading and thought, and I have offered them seriously; but I am aware that a full defense of them would require more time. However, let me call the reader's attention to this: if I seem to be attempting to instigate a revolution, it is merely in critical thinking and is not in the practice of literature. The epic and the poetic drama, for example, have long been dead, and I did not kill them. I have merely tried to account for their death, and to express my belief that the fault is not with us but is in the nature of the forms. The novel, for the most part an abortive form from its beginnings, is dying rapidly; but here I think that the fault is with us—with the novelists and the critics. The writers of the short poem have done very well, if one regards them over a long period, and they are definitely alive today; but I am convinced that greater achievements are possible in the short poem and that we would have a better chance of such achievements if we could bring ourselves to understand the nature of the form and the fact that this form is the greatest form, of all forms the one most suited to communication among those who are wholly civilized and adult.

I have tried to indicate the kinds of problem which must be studied if we are to estimate the possibilities of any of the forms, and some of the most pressing problems in connection with each form. I may be wrong in any or all of my particular conclusions, but if I am wrong it will have to be demonstrated by argument. If my arguments are merely brushed aside, I shall win by default within twenty years. If I am right, there will be no great harm in this, and it will not be the first time I have won an argument in this manner; but if I am wrong, it will be unfortunate.

FOOTNOTES

[1]The reader curious about Babbitt's positive program, that which he opposed to Romanticism, should turn to the "Introduction" to *Democracy and Leadership*. That which is specifically human in man, and ultimately divine, we learn, is the higher will, or will to refrain. This is opposed to the lower will, or expansive appetite. Babbitt gives the will primacy over the intellect and over the emotions. But the will must have standards: it does not occur to Babbitt that he is now giving standards primacy over the will. Standards, in turn, are derived by the imagination, which sees likenesses and analogies, in connection with the power which discriminates. These last two powers in conjunction would seem to be nothing more nor less than a new description of the discursive reason. Why Babbitt did not choose to face this fact and admit the primacy of reason, I do not know. But this reason, one should note, provides standards merely for the will to refrain: the expansive will is unguided; it is merely checked from time to time. There would seem to be no explicit ethics of positive action, and this defect is more obvious in Babbitt's friend Paul Elmer More, in whom the only good is renunciation and inaction.

[2]I have in mind a man two or three years younger than myself, one of the most promising men of my generation. He took an M.A. at Stanford and a Ph.D. at the University of California. He was an instructor for three years at Harvard. He then retired to an orange and olive ranch in the southern San Joaquin valley, and has remained there since. He had published, during the years of his activity, a fine collection of poems, a promising first novel, and a valuable book on Elizabethan tragedy.

[3]See the following publications: *The Well-Wrought Urn,* by Cleanth Brooks, Reynal and Hitchcock, 1947; R. S. Crane: *Cleanth Brooks; or, The Bankruptcy of Critical Monism,* Modern Philology 45 (May 1948). This last, with modifications, is reprinted in *Critics and Criticism,* University of Chicago Press, 1952, an anthology of the Chicago Critics, edited by Crane. All references to Crane in this essay are to his contributions to this volume and to

his *The Languages of Criticism and the Structure of Poetry*, University of Toronto Press, 1953.

[4]See *A Critic's Job of Work*, in *Language as Gesture*, by R. P. Backmur, Harcourt Brace and Company, 1952.

[5]*Reason in Madness*, by Allen Tate, G. P. Putnam's Sons, 1941.

[6]See *Logic and Lyric*, by J. V. Cunningham, *Modern Philology*, Vol. LI, No. 1, Aug. 1953.

[7]For a very clear but brief account of associationism in the eighteenth century, see *John Keats' Fancy*, by J. R. Caldwell, Cornell University Press, Chapter Two. For a more detailed account, combined with an account of the influence of Shaftesbury and of allied matters, see *From Classic to Romantic*, by Walter Jackson Bate, Harvard University Press.

[8]*Woe or Wonder: The Emotional Effect of Shakespearian Tragedy* by J. V. Cunningham, the University of Denver Press, 1951.

[9]*The Wife of Martin Guerre*, by Janet Lewis, The Colt Press, 1941; reissued in *Anchor in the Sea*, edited by Alan Swallow, The Swallow Press and William Morrow and Company, 1947; reissued as a separate book by Alan Swallow, Denver, 1950; translated into French by Françoise O. Jobit and published as *La Femme de Martin Guerre*, by Robert Laffont, Paris, 1947.

[10]I have recently received an advertising circular from the College Department of Harper and Brothers which announces a new edition of *The Ambassadors*, in which the reversed chapters will be put back in their proper order. The correction is attributed to the two articles which I have mentioned.

[11]The essay appears in *Axel's Castle* (1931), and is reprinted in *Literary Opinion in America*, edited by M. D. Zabel (revised edition), 1951.

[12]*The Puritan Mind*, by H. W. Schneider (Henry Holt, 1930) page 48. This and other passages of a similar nature are quoted in my essay on Hawthorne (*In Defense of Reason*). They are applied by Schneider to the colonial Puritans. I suppose that in any allegory, universals will creep in somewhere: Ahab, in *Moby Dick*, represents the soul per se, Fedallah the predestined sinning will in Edwards' terms and the characterizing mind in Melville's, and Starbuck represents unaided virtue, or reason unsupported by Grace. But the whale himself, as the spirit of evil, is less a universal than a unique phenomenon, and so are most of the other details: the warnings, allurements, and the like. The Calvinists

themselves could not get rid of universals entirely, for as theologians they had to talk in terms of them; but they did their best. And they were successful to the point that they produced a state of mind that would have seemed strange to Dante and Aquinas.

[13]The recovery is occasional in most of these poets, and where it occurs is probably due more to critical tact than to theory. With Cunningham and Bowers, however, it is due to both; they know precisely what they are doing, and the result is remarkable.

[14]A brief word of warning should be introduced here regarding expository poetry. If the poet undertakes a subject which calls for a great deal of meticulous argument, metaphysical, religious, political or other, in order to reach the generalizations having some kind of important human significance, he is again invading the area of prose. Pope's *Essay on Man* is an example: even if we grant the validity of his argument—which would be foolish—the poem fails for this reason, and is impressive only in short passages. Dryden, in *The Hind and the Panther,* tried to evade this difficulty by the use of a preposterous allegory. The poem contains a passage of fine, though not quite first-rate devotional poetry, beginning with line 62 and fading out toward 84; but the passage is inferior to the best of Jonson, Donne, and the Herberts, and is not separable; and the whole poem is dull. In brief, there are certain materials which are proper to expository prose but improper to expository verse, just as there are materials proper to narrative prose but improper to narrative verse. For example, it would have been a mistake to write this essay in verse.

[15]This poem, which appears to me obviously one of Stevens' half-dozen greatest, and perhaps the best of those, appeared in *The Hudson Review* for the Spring of 1951 (Vol. IV, No. I). Stevens did not see fit to include it in his *Collected Poems.*

[16]In *Le Cimetière Marin,* Valéry is unmistakably the speaker, and there is no dramatic intermediary. The Sun is the image of the First Cause, and is not, as in the *Serpent,* the accomplice of the speaker. Valéry addresses the Sun in much the same terms used by the Serpent in addressing the Creator:

> L'âme exposée aux torches du solstice,
> Je te soutiens, admirable justice
> De la lumière aux armes sans pitié!
> Je te rends pure à ta place première:

> Regarde-toi! . . . Mais rendre la lumière
> Suppose d'ombre une morne moitié.

Compare this passage with stanza eight, lines five, six and seven, of the *Serpent* which I shall quote later. Consider also:

> Tu n'as que moi pour contenir tes craintes!
> Mes repentirs, mes doutes, mes contraintes
> Sont le défaut de ton grand diamant.

The theme of this poem again is the flaw in the creation. The particular aspect of the flaw upon which the poem concentrates is the insolubility of the mystery of discontinuity, which we encounter in the act of creation (Entre le vide et l'évènement pure) and in the mystery of death, and the emphasis in most of the poem is on death, although the address to Zeno near the conclusion emphasizes the mystery of change as change. Like the *Serpent*, this poem emphasizes the torture of life on these terms (Amour, peut-être, ou de moi-même haine?) and rejects immortality on these terms (Maigre immortalité noire et dorée). Unlike the *Serpent* it asserts in the last stanzas the necessity of continuing to live in the time allotted us. Such an assertion would be superfluous in the *Serpent*, for the Serpent, as myth on the one hand, or as the figurative representative of the mind of man on the other, is immortal in any event. That is the final horror of his situation.

The Audible Reading

of Poetry

My title may seem to have in it something of the jargon of the modern Educationist; if so, I am sorry, but I mean to indicate something more than the reading of poetry aloud. I mean to indicate the reading of poetry not merely for the sensual ear, but for the mind's ear as well; yet the mind's ear can be trained only by way of the other, and the matter, practically considered, comes inescapably back to the reading of poetry aloud.

It is also important to learn to read prose aloud, and to hear the prose when one reads it silently. Melville, Gibbon, or Samuel Johnson about equally will be lost on us if we do not so hear it. Yet the readers are numerous who hear nothing when they read silently and who are helpless in their efforts to read aloud: some of them have defective sensibilities; some have merely never been trained; some have been trained by one or another of our psychological educationalists to read in this fashion in order that they may read more rapidly. That they can read more rapidly without hearing, I believe there is no doubt, especially if the matter with which they are dealing is trivial. The trouble is that the activity cannot properly be called reading. Such "readers" are barbarians; literature is closed to them, in spite of the fact that they may think otherwise. The scholar who appears to have read everything has commonly understood very little, and his failure to hear is one of the reasons.

My subject may seem a bit precious and tenuous, but it is neither; it is a matter of the utmost importance to the proper understanding of poetry, a matter fully as important as the philosophical speculation and learned paraphrasing of the New Critics, of whom I am sometimes reputed to be one. It is a matter of which there is almost no understanding at the present time.

Poetry, as nearly as I can understand it, is a statement in words about a human experience, whether the experience be real or hypothetical, major or minor; but it is a statement of a particular kind. Words are symbols for concepts, and the philosopher or scientist endeavors as far as may be to use them with reference to nothing save their conceptual content. Most words, however, connote feelings and perceptions, and the poet, like the writer of imaginative prose, endeavors to use them with reference not only to their denotations but to their connotations as well. Such writers endeavor to communicate not only concepts, arranged, presumably, either in rational order or in an order apprehensible by the rational mind, but the feeling or emotion which the rational content ought properly to arouse. The poet differs from the writer of any kind of prose in that he writes in metrical language. Any good prose is rhythmical up to a certain point: even purely expository prose should be rhythmical to the point that audible obstructions are minimized and meanings are emphasized; the prose of such a writer as Melville is far more elaborately rhythmical than this. But a rhythm which is not controlled by a definite measure will be relatively loose and lacking in subtlety. Poetry and music are based upon definite measure; in this they differ from all other forms of composition.

Rhythm and meter, it should be observed, are quite distinct from each other, in spite of the fact that many critics (myself among them) sometimes use the two words as if they meant the same thing. Meter is the arithmetical norm, the purely theoretic structure of the line; rhythm is controlled departure from that norm. The iambic pentameter norm, for example, proceeds as follows:

One *two,* one *two,* one *two,* one *two,* one *two.*

Yet no other line in the language corresponds exactly to the line just given; and to achieve another as regular one will have to resort to the same repetitive structure with a new pair of syllables. Every other line will depart from this one for these reasons: no two syllables ever have the same degree of accent—that is, so far as versification is concerned there is no such thing as an inherently accented or unaccented syllable, but syllables which count technically as accented can be recognized as such only with reference to the other syllable or syllables within the same foot: secondly, although quantity or syllable-length has no part in the measure, it is, like accent, infinitely variable and it affects the rhythm; and thirdly, feet of other types may be substituted for iambic feet, at least within reason. As I have said, rhythm results from the proper control and manipulation of these sources of variation.

Now rhythm is in a measure expressive of emotion. If the poet, then, is endeavoring to make a statement in which rational understanding and emotion are properly related to each other, metrical language will be of the greatest advantage to him, for it will provide him with a means of qualifying his emotion more precisely than he could otherwise do, of adjusting it more finely to the rational understanding which gives rise to it. The rational and emotional contents of the poem thus exist simultaneously, from moment to moment, in the poem; they are not distinct, but are separable only by analysis; the poet is not writing in language which was first conceptual and then emotionalized, nor in prose which has been metered; he is writing in poetical language. And the rhythm of the poem permeates the entire poem as pervasively as blood permeates the human body: remove it and you have a corpse. It is for this reason that the audible reading of poetry is quite as important as the philosophical understanding of poetry; without audible reading, and adequate audible reading, you simply do not have poetry.

We are thus confronted with the question of what constitutes adequate audible reading. From what I have just said, it should be obvious that adequate audible reading will be reading in which the rhythm of the poem is rendered intact, without the sacrifice of any other element. But what variety of reading will best achieve this end, and what are some of the problems which arise in connection with it?

Since I am defending an unpopular cause, I shall not scruple to avail myself of eminent support. In looking over the *Selected Writings* of Paul Valéry recently issued by New Directions, I found Valéry writing as follows:

. . . . in studying a piece of poetry one intends to recite, one should not take as source or point of departure ordinary conversation and common parlance, in order to rise from this level of prose to the desired poetic tone: but, on the contrary, I thought one should take song as a base, and should put oneself in the state of a singer; adjust one's voice to the plenitude of musical sound, and from there descend to the somewhat less resonant state suitable to verse. This, it seemed to me, was the only way to preserve the musical essence of poems. Above all, the voice must be placed quite away from prose, and the text studied from the point of view of necessary attack, modulation, sustained tone, little by little, lowering this musical disposition, which in the beginning one has exaggerated, to bring it down to the proportions of poetry. . . . above all do not be in a hurry to arrive at the meaning. Approach it without effort and, as it were, insensibly. And only in or by means of the music attain to tenderness or to violence. . . . Remain in this pure musical state until such time as the meaning, appearing little by little, can no longer mar the musical form. You will introduce it at the end as the supreme nuance that will transfigure the passage without altering it.[1]

This appears to be a plea for a restrained but formal chant, in which a sustained tone and movement will serve as an impersonal but definite base for subtle variation. It is only by such a reading, for example, that *Le Cimetière Marin* can be rendered; it is only by a man who so read that such a poem could have been written.

A poem in the very nature of the case is a formal statement; and the reading of a poem is thus a formal occasion. A poem is not conversation; neither is it drama. Conversation is in general the least premeditated and least rhythmical of human utterance; and it depends very heavily upon intonations and even gestures and facial expressions which are not at the disposal of the poet. Dramatic speech is merely more or less formalized conversation. Dramatic poetry, of course, presents a special problem, and one with which I shall not at present concern myself, though it is closer to the kind of poetry with which I am dealing than it is to dramatic prose, and I agree with Valéry that it is commonly botched by the actors. I have never witnessed a performance of Shakespeare without more of pain than of profit or of pleasure. I have been repeatedly reminded of a story told by W. B. Yeats of the great

Shakespearian actor of whom it was said that he read Shakespeare so beautifully that no one could tell it was poetry. In general I think the world would be well enough off without actors: they appear to be capable of any of three feats—of making the grossly vulgar appear acceptably mediocre; of making the acceptably mediocre appear what it is; and of making the distinguished appear acceptably mediocre. In any event, they cannot read poetry, for they try to make it appear to be something else, something, in brief, which they themselves can understand.

A poem calls for a formal reading, partly because the poem itself is of its own nature a formal statement, and partly because only such a reading will render the rhythm with precision. Furthermore, it is only with a formal tone as a basis that variations of tone within the poem can be rendered with precision: without such a formal tone to unify the poem, the poem becomes merely a loose assortment of details. The situation here is precisely analogous to that which I have described elsewhere[2] with regard to rhythm and meter: the firmer the metric structure, the more precise can be the rhythmic variations, and the greater the effect obtainable with a very slight variation; whereas if the structure is loose the variations lack significance.

A formal reading which avoids dramatic declamation will necessarily take on something of the nature of a chant. This kind of reading itself has dangers, however, for the reader may carry the procedure so far as to appear precious, and worse, he may deform syllables in the interests of what he considers musical intonation, much as a musical composer will draw syllables out or hurry over them in setting a poem to music. I never heard the late W. B. Yeats read aloud, but I have been told that he was guilty of both of these vices: if it is true that he was guilty of them, one has some reason to suspect that he never properly heard his own poems, a fact which may have been responsible for a number of curious rhythmical mishaps which are scattered through his works. A poem should, on the contrary, be conceived as having a movement of its own, an autonomous movement, which should be rendered as purely and as impersonally as possible. The reader has no more right to revise the rhythms in the interest of what he considers an effective presentation than he has a right to revise any other aspects of the language. The poem, once set in motion, should appear to move of its own momentum.

A more or less recent poet who went farther than any other has gone in deforming the inherent rhythmic elements in our language and so rendering the structure of his poems indecipherable is Gerard Manley Hopkins. Hopkins held a theory of dramatic or declamatory reading, and I suspect from a few passages in his prose that he combined this with a theory of musical intonation. Hopkins was an eccentric and extremely egoistic man, and he worked in isolation. He apparently failed to realize that his own dramatic and musical deformations of language were not based on universal principles but were purely private. As a result one can often be only dumfounded when he indicates his intentions by metrical signs, and one can often be only baffled when he fails to do so. In *Spelt from Sibyl's Leaves,* for example, Hopkins uses an extremely long line, which, if it is read with normal accentuation, produces the effect of a loosely irregular but still readable verse. He does not provide us with many accent marks until he is about halfway through the poem; from there on he provides marks in abundance, frequently with strange results. The last two lines will serve as illustration:

> But thése two; wáre of a wórld where bút these / twó tell,
>> each óff the óther; of a rack
>
> Where, selfwrung, selfstrung, sheathe- and shelterless, /
>> thóughts agaínst thoughts ín groans grínd.

We have here a kind of bad writing which is purely the result of bad reading; and even the best reading, if superimposed upon what the poet offers, can salvage the poem but very imperfectly.

In T. S. Eliot's reading of *The Waste Land,* as we have it on the recordings issued by The Library of Congress, we have another kind of dramatic reading, and conceivably a relationship between the way of reading and the way of writing. In those portions which exhibit a more or less definite rhythmic structure—for example, in *Death by Water*—Eliot reads more or less in the fashion which I am recommending, with a minimum of dramatic improvement on the text, and with a maximum of attention to movement. But in those portions of the poem—and they are the greater part of it—in which the rhythm does not cohere, in which the poem tends to fall apart in sandy fragments, Eliot reads dramatically; he does this with a good deal of skill, but most of what he puts into his voice is not in the poem—he descends to the practice of the actor who is salvaging a weak text. It would be interesting to know whether Eliot devised this mode of reading in order to rescue a weak poem, or whether the weak poem resulted in part from his having come gradually to employ such a mode of reading, so that he tended to see in his text as he was composing it something which he was not actually getting down on paper. This latter procedure in any event probably accounts for a good deal of the unrealized poetry of our time. For example, Randal Jarrell's reading of his poem *Lady Bates*, in The Library of Congress series, is very dramatic, very emotional, and very bad: I am unable to hear it without the conviction that Jarrell felt his emotions about his subject so readily and so uncritically that he did not trouble himself to write the poem. The poem itself is formless and dull.

The dependence upon superimposed rhythms or other effects which we get in a grotesque form in some of Hopkins and in a more skillful form in Eliot's reading of *The Waste Land* can lead to an astonishing degree of imperception on the part of critics (which is merely an impressive way of saying on the part of readers). In the volume entitled *Gerard Manley Hopkins,* by the Kenyon Critics, Mr. Harold Whitehall informs us that from about the year 1300 English poetry has become less and less amenable to being read aloud, because less and less rhythmical. And in another volume on Hopkins, edited by Norman Weyand, S.J., and written by a group of Jesuits, a volume entitled *Immortal Diamond,* Walter J. Ong arrives at similar conclusions. Both of these writers believe that there is no real rhythm without heavy stress; both believe that meter is based on·declamatory rather than mechanical stress. Ong gives us no clue as to how we are to recognize our stressed syllables, and he fails to explain how Hopkins arrived at any of the stresses which he marked. Whitehall gives us his own system of stressing Hopkins, but it is quite as arbitrary as that of Hopkins, and when Whitehall's marked passages are finished we are left with no means of proceeding. Ong, convinced that there is no fine rhythm without heavy and obvious stress, is oblivious of the sensitivity of Sidney and the post-Sidneyan metrists, and equally of the structural principles of their verse; and his concept of reading aloud is indicated by the following passage: "If the poem calls for shouting, the shouting need not be kept imaginary for fear the beat of the rhythm will go. Shout, declaim, and you will only have thrust this rhythm home. So, too, if the shout should need to die to a whisper . . ." This clerical type of rendition strikes me as about equally impractical, insensitive, and indecorous.

Nevertheless, rhetorical stress has a certain relationship to the structure of meter, but it is not the relationship sought by Hopkins. As I have already said, the language does not divide itself evenly into accented and unaccented syllables, but there is almost infinite variation in degrees of accent. For this reason, the basic rule of English scansion is this: that the accented syllable can be determined only in relationship to the other syllable or syllables within the same foot. The accented syllable of a given foot, as we shall eventually see, may be one of the lightest syllables in its line. But with this rule as a reservation, we may go on to say that poetic meter must be constructed out of the inherent (or mechanical) accentual materials of the language, so that the accented syllable of a foot will be naturally heavier than the unaccented; and if the poet desires to indicate a rhetorical stress he should do it by a metrical stress, or if he is using two syllables either of which might receive heavier stress than the other, then the rhetorical stress should fall where the reader as a result of the previously established pattern will expect the metrical stress.

Keats neglects these considerations in the first line of his last sonnet. The inexpert reader who endeavors to render this line conversationally or dramatically will read it as if he were a sociable lady addressing another sociable lady at a party:

Bright star,   would *I* were steadfast   as *thou* art,

88

and the rhythm is destroyed along with the possibility of a proper rhyme. The fault, however, lies largely with Keats. It is natural to stress the two contrasting pronouns somewhat, although one need not carry the stress all the way to the ridiculous. Furthermore, on the first pronoun the metrical stress indicates the rhetorical, so that the two are not in conflict. If we consider the words *Would I* in isolation, we shall see that so far as their mechanical properties are concerned, either can be stressed at the expense of the other; however, in this line the stressing of *would* would result in an inverted foot in the second position, and although inversion is possible in this position, it is difficult and generally unlikely, so that we naturally expect the stress to fall on *I*, which likewise is the natural recipient of the rhetorical stress. If we employ the four words *Would I were steadfast* in isolation, the stress may fall variously according to our meaning. If we are implying a contrast between steadfastness and our lack of it, the heaviest stress falls on *would;* if we are implying a contrast between steadfastness and another particular quality, a light stress falls on *would* and a heavy on *stead-;* if we are implying a contrast between our own lack of steadfastness and the steadfastness of another, the heavy stress falls on *I,* as in the actual line, but if, as in this line, the comparison is completed, an equal stress should fall on the second pronoun; but since this pronoun also is coupled with a verb which is mechanically its equal and on the basis of its inherent nature could as well take the accent, and since the foot ends the line, and a rhymed line at that, the accent must fall on *art.* This blunder by Keats could scarcely have occurred as a result of his reading poetry in a dramatic fashion, for he understood the structure of English poetry very well, and had he read the line dramatically he would have noticed the error. It probably occurred as a result of his reading with a somewhat mechanical scansion, so that he failed to observe that the meaning was struggling with the meter. One can read it, of course, by means of a more or less evasive glide, but it constitutes an unhappy moment.

One can observe a related difficulty in the sixth line of Wordsworth's sonnet *Upon Westminster Bridge*:

> Ships, towers, domes, theatres, and temples lie.

The first four words of this line are coördinate in grammatical function and in importance, and in ordinary prose the first four syllables would be indistinguishable to the ear in the matter of accent. The average reader, if asked to mark the scansion of this poem, will indicate two spondees at the beginning of the line, but the first two feet are not spondaic—in spite of everything they are iambic. The truly spondaic foot is extremely rare in English; presently I shall have occasion to illustrate it, but for the present I shall merely describe it. It can occur as a variant in iambic verse, only if the accented syllables in the iambic feet are heavily accented and the unaccented are very light, and only if the cesural pause is heavily marked; and these conditions must prevail not merely in the line in question, but throughout much of the poem. The true spondee is a violent aberration—it is a form of what Hopkins calls sprung rhythm—and it is possible only where the rhythm is heavy and obvious. It can be found at least as early as Barnabe Googe and as late as the songbooks of John Dowland, and within these limits it may conceivably be found in as many as thirty poems, but I think it will be difficult to find it elsewhere except in the work of Gerard Hopkins, although something approaching it occurs occasionally in Henry Vaughan. In this sonnet by Wordsworth an extremely smooth iambic movement has been established in the first five lines, so effectively established that it dominates the sixth line, and almost any reader who is aware of rhythm at all will be forced to impose a very light iambic emphasis on the first two feet of the sixth line; to do otherwise will bring the poem apart in ruins. This can be done; but the difficulty indicates a defect in the poem, and a defect again which probably stems from faulty reading on the part of the poet. The difficulty is enhanced by the length of the syllables (a length increased by the commas) and by the all but insufferable series of dentals.

The relationship of rhetorical stress to metrical stress, and hence to reading, would appear, then, to be real, although the relationship can obviously be abused. Perhaps I should conclude the matter by offering these rules for poet and reader alike: (1) There should be no conflict between rhetorical stress and metrical stress, but insofar as it is possible the metrical stress should point the meaning; (2) where the mechanical potentialities of the language indicate the possibility of a stress in either of two directions, the grammatical structure should be so definite that a certain rhetorical stress will be unmistakable and will force the metrical interpretation in the right direction; and (3) the reader should deal with rhetorical stresses with the utmost restraint—he should indicate them as far as the occasion requires, but he should not become enthusiastic, undignified, or unmetrical about them. They are not to be superimposed upon the basic rhythm, nor can the basic rhythm be constructed from them.

I would like next to illustrate the importance of reading, by illustrating certain very marked differences in rhythm which may occur within the limits of the iambic pentameter line. English verse is predominantly iambic in structure, and although this fact has irritated certain poets and stirred them to curious experiments, the fact that so vast a number of eminent poets have found the iambic movement more useful than any other must have some kind of explanation. In the anapestic or dactyllic foot the accented syllable must be definitely heavy or the identity of the foot and of the line will disappear, and this necessity makes for monotony and a jingling obviousness:

> I sprang to the stirrup, and Joris, and he;
> I galloped, Dirck galloped, we galloped all three. . . .

The unequivocally trochaic line tends to exhibit some of the same heaviness (as in *Hiawatha,* for example) although the reason for this is less clear. The seven-syllable tetrameter line may be described as trochaic, with a monosyllabic foot in the last position, or as iambic with a monosyllabic foot in the first position; since it is frequently used as a variant on iambic tetrameter, the second classification would seem the better. When this line is used throughout a poem, the poem will be short, or else will become monotonous: the accents again are usually heavy most of the time, and although the meter may be used in a short poem for the purpose of obtaining a didactic or

91

semi-songlike effect, it appears to have few other uses. The iambic movement, however, appears to be natural to the language; it asserts itself easily, and the poet does not have to hammer his accents out to maintain it. This situation allows the poet to vary the degrees of his accents widely, to vary his cesuras, and to employ substitution with a certain freedom. Contrary to the views of Mr. Whitehall and of Father Ong, this type of meter lends itself very well to audible reading, but one must first know how to read. And when well written and well read it is far more flexible and perceptive than any other kind of English verse thus far devised.

My first example is by Barnabe Googe and was written early in the reign of Elizabeth, before the advent of Spenser and Sidney:

> Give money me, take friendship who so list,
> For friends are gone, come once adversity,
> When money yet remaineth safe in chest
> That quickly can thee bring from misery;
> Fair face show friends, when riches do abound,
> Come time of proof, farewell they must away;
> Believe me well, they are not to be found,
> If God but send thee once a lowering day.
> Gold never starts aside, but in distress,
> Finds ways enough to ease thine heaviness.

This poem has certain characteristics which one would expect to find in a period in which the pentameter line was new, when the misunderstandings of Wyatt had been only recently overcome: first of all there are no inverted feet and no trisyllabic feet; secondly the accented syllables are almost all heavy and of nearly the same weight—there are only two feet in the poem in which the accented syllables are noticeably light; thirdly the cesuras are all heavily marked, and in six of the ten lines they fall at the end of the second foot. The poem shows only one type of metrical variation; that is, the use of spondaic feet (or what I have elsewhere called syllabic sprung meter). The introduction of this variation into the newly acquired iambic pentameter line is Googe's principle contribution to the technique of English verse, and it is a contribution of no mean importance. There are two spondees at the beginning of line five; there is one at the beginning of six;

there is one at the beginning of nine; and the first foot of the last line may be read with equal success as a spondee or as an iamb. All of these spondees can be forced into the iambic pattern, but they will have to be forced, and the poem will suffer. It is only in a poem such as this one, in which the rhythm is strongly and obviously marked by a great and regular distinction between accented and unaccented syllables that the true spondee can occur; in a smoother and subtler type of structure, such as my next example, two syllables of nearly the same degree of accent will be absorbed into the iambic pattern and will not stand out as approximately equal to each other; furthermore, any attempt to read them as spondees will destroy the movement of the poem.

My next example is from Shakespeare. Before this sonnet was written, Sidney and other early experimenters had rendered the line smoother, more varied, and more subtle:

> When to the sessions of sweet silent thought
> I summon up remembrance of things past,
> I sigh the lack of many a thing I sought,
> And with old woes new wail my dear time's waste:
> Then can I drown an eye unused to flow,
> For precious friends, hid in death's dateless night,
> And weep afresh love's long-since-cancelled woe,
> And moan th'expense of many a vanish'd sight:
> Then can I grieve at grievances foregone,
> And heavily from woe to woe tell o'er
> The sad account of fore-bemoaned moan
> Which I new pay as if not paid before.
>   But if the while I think on thee, dear friend,
>   All losses are restored and sorrows end.

The position of the cesura in this sonnet is less varied than in the poem by Googe; it falls after the second foot in eleven out of fourteen lines; but the cesura is much less noticeable, partly because it is not emphasized by heavy grammatical breaks, and partly because of other qualities of the rhythm. Aside from this difference in cesural value, the most considerable rhythmic difference between this poem and the poem by Googe resides in the fact that there are great differences in the degrees of accent to be found *among the syllables which count metrically as accented.* It will be remembered that I remarked earlier that the accented syllable can be recognized as such only with reference to the other syllable or syllables within the same foot, for no two syllables bear exactly the same degree of accent: it is this fact which gives the rhythm of the best English verse its extreme sensitivity. But rhythm, in poetry as in music, is controlled variation from an arithmetical norm; and the rhythm ceases to be rhythm, and becomes merely movement, whenever the norm itself is no longer discernible.

I will illustrate what I have been saying by two lines from the sonnet. The scansion of the first line gives us a trochee followed by four iambs. The third foot, however, which is composed of the second syllable of *sessions* followed by the preposition *of* (the accented syllable), is very lightly accented. In the following foot, which is composed of *sweet,* followed by the first syllable of *silent, sweet,* the unaccented syllable, is more heavily stressed than the accented syllable of the preceding foot, so that we have in effect a series of four degrees of accent within two successive feet. Furthermore, if the reader should suffer from the delusion (a common one) that the second of these feet is really a spondee, let him read it the way he is forced to read the true spondees in the poem by Googe, and he will discover that spondaic rhythm is a very different matter from what he has here, and that the attempt to introduce it into this poem will be disastrous. The same thing occurs in the fourth and fifth feet of line nine:

> Then can I grieve at grievances foregone.

It occurs in the first two feet of Bryant's line:

> Where thy pale form was laid with many tears.

It occurs in the last two feet of Ben Jonson's line:

> Drink to me only with thine eyes.

It is, in fact, one of the commonest phenomena in English verse, yet I have seen a good many distinguished scholars and eminent poets interpret it wrongly.

I shall now quote a well known song from John Dowland's *Second Book of Aires*:

Fine knacks for ladies, cheap, choice, brave and new!
  Good pennyworths! but money cannot move.
I keep a fair but for the fair to view;
  A beggar may be liberal of love.
Though all my wares be trash, the heart is true.

Great gifts are guiles and look for gifts again;
  My trifles come as treasures from my mind.
It is a precious jewel to be plain;
  Sometimes in shell the Orient's pearls we find.
Of others take a sheaf, of me a grain.

Within this pack, pins, points, laces, and gloves,
  And divers toys, fitting a country fair.
But my heart lives where duty serves and loves,
  Turtles and twins, court's brood, a heavenly pair.
Happy the heart that thinks of no removes.

There are sprung, or spondaic, feet in the first, second, sixth, seventh, eleventh, thirteenth, and fourteenth lines of this poem. These feet represent the same kind of variant which we found in Googe, and for the most part we have the same strongly marked difference between accented and unaccented syllables and similarly strong cesural pauses, even in lines in which no spondees occur. Yet whereas the rhythm of Googe is hard, fast, and didactic, the rhythm of this poem is slower, more complicated, and very songlike. The result is partly due to more spondaic variants than we found in Googe, and to spondaic variants in other positions than the initial ones; it is partly due to the introduction at certain points of the type of line which we found in Shakespeare, such as the following:

It is a precious jewel to be plain.

a line in which the iambic fourth foot, composed of the second syllable of *jewel* and the preposition *to*, is extremely light and short and is followed by a final foot (*be plain*) in which the unaccented syllable is heavier than the accented syllable *to* before it; yet in this last foot the difference between *be* and *plain* is so marked that no one would be tempted to call the foot a spondee.

The author likewise does certain strange and ingenious things with his spondees. The first line, for example, goes as follows:

Fine knacks for ladies, cheap, choice, brave and new!

The first foot is spondaic, the second iambic; the third foot, consisting of the second syllable of *ladies* and of *cheap,* is likewise iambic, but the cesura, reinforced by the comma, in mid-foot, throws the accent onto *cheap* with unusual force, and *cheap* is then followed by the spondaic foot consisting of two syllables which are almost exactly equal to it, and which are likewise set off by commas, so that we have the illusion of a foot consisting of three accented syllables, or an English molossus. The author does something similar but almost more adventurous in the eleventh line, where the heavily iambic foot *this pack* is followed by the heavy spondee *pins, points,* which in turn is followed by the heavily inverted foot, *laces,* with the result that we get four strong accents in sequence, though only one spondee. Technically, this is one of the most brilliant poems in the language. Dowland (or his unknown poet) learned what he could from Googe and improved upon it; and he complicated the method (without destroying it—a difficult feat) by rhythms acquired from the refiners of the intervening period.

I shall now show the use of different types of iambic pentameter rhythm employed in a regular pattern. To do this, I shall employ a song by Campion. The song rhymes in couplets. The metric pattern begins with two lines of what one might call the primitive type, with heavy stresses and heavy cesuras, but with no spondees: in these two lines the first and third feet are inverted, the rest iambic, and the cesura falls after the second foot. The third and fifth lines are evenly iambic and are less heavily stressed, and the cesuras in these lines occur in different positions and are so light as to be all but imperceptible. The fourth and sixth lines are of the same type of iambic movement as the last lines mentioned, but contain seven feet instead of five. There are two stanzas, and the pattern in the two is as nearly identical as the inescapable variations of language permit:

Follow your saint, follow with accents sweet!
Haste you, sad notes, fall at her flying feet!
There, wrapt in cloud of sorrow, pity move,
And tell the ravisher of my soul I perish for her love:
But if she scorns my never ceasing pain,
Then burst with sighing in her sight, and ne'er return again.

All that I sung still to her praise did tend;
Still she was first, still she my songs did end;
Yet she my love and music both doth fly,
The music that her echo is and beauty's sympathy:
Then let my notes pursue her scornful flight!
It shall suffice that they were breathed and died for her delight.

I shall now quote a sonnet by Gerard Hopkins, which is basically iambic pentameter, but which employs every conceivable variant. I have marked and described the scansion of this sonnet in
my essay on Hopkins, and at this time I shall make only a few general remarks about the structure. The poem contains iambic feet,
trochees, spondees, one molossus (a foot of three accented syllables), monosyllabic feet, trisyllabic feet of one accent each, and
one or two feet which must be considered either as containing
more than three syllables or else as containing syllables which are
extrametrical or elided. The poem is successful as regards structure and rhythm, and it offers a rhythmic departure from the
norm about as extreme as anyone is likely to achieve:

No worst, there is none. Pitched past pitch of grief,
More pangs will, schooled at forepangs, wilder wring.
Comforter, where, where is your comforting?
Mary, mother of us, where is your relief?
My cries heave, herds-long; huddle in a main, a chief
Woe, world sorrow; on an age-old anvil wince and sing—
Then lull, then leave off. Fury had shrieked 'No ling-
ering! Let me be fell: force I must be brief.'

O the mind, mind has mountains; cliffs of fall
Frightful, sheer, no-man-fathomed. Hold them cheap
May who ne'er hung there. Nor does long our small
Durance deal with that steep or deep. Here! creep,

> Wretch under a comfort serves in a whirlwind: all
> Life death does end and each day dies with sleep.

By the use of five short poems I have indicated a number of widely varying rhythms all of which are measured by iambic pentameter. So far as meter and rhythm are concerned all five are masterpieces; and in spite of any faults which may be found in them with regard to other matters, all five are brilliant poems and should be part of the literary experience of any man using the English language. Yet not one of these poems amounts to anything if its rhythm is not rendered with great precision; to read the poem so that its rhythm does not emerge in its totality and in every detail is to reduce the poem to lifeless fragments. You cannot buy expert readings of these poems on disks, as you can buy expert renderings of Bach and Mozart; nor can you go to a concert and hear them—every man is his own performer. It is important, therefore, that one read properly. But to read properly one must understand the principles both of English meter and of English rhythm, and not in a haphazard manner, but precisely; and one must understand the use of one's own voice; and after that one must practice.

I am at a disadvantage in dealing with a subject of this kind before an audience whom I cannot reach with my voice, for I cannot demonstrate, but am forced to try to describe. The nearest thing to a demonstration that I can offer is my reading of my own poems in the Library of Congress series. I do not consider myself a finished performer, nor, I think, are these readings the best of which I am capable. But they are all I can offer, and they will serve to indicate the method in a general way.

I have been told that this method of reading makes all poems sound alike, but this can be true only for those persons to whom all poems sound alike in any event, or for whom essential differences are meaningless. The virtue of the method, on the contrary, is that it gives each poem its precise identity, and no other method will do this. If this precise identity does not interest you, then you are not interested in poetry and you will in all likelihood never discover poetry. Some time ago, when I was defending this method of reading in public, a well-known scholar objected to my theories with a good deal of indignation, and he objected especially to my reading of the Dowland poem which I have quoted in these pages. He said that it was a street song, or peddler's song, and should be rendered as such. I do not know exactly how Elizabethan street songs were rendered, and I do not believe that he knew; but any attempt so to render it would be, I am sure, unfortunate, even if one had the necessary information. The poem is not a street song; it is a poem on love and on the art of poetry and on a relationship between the two, and it is one of the most deeply serious and deeply moving short poems in the Elizabethan period—the peddler is purely metaphorical, and his part in the poem is both indicated and formalized by the metrical structure and it should remain formal and no more than indicated in the reading. If the poet refers by way of metaphor to a cow, the reader is not, I trust, expected to moo. I refer the reader back to my quotations from Valéry, especially the last sentence. Of the "meaning" of the poem he says: "You will introduce it at the end as the supreme nuance that will transfigure the poem without altering it." By "the end," he means the end of the process of studying the poem and arriving at the proper rendering.

Bad reading and bad (or no) training in metrical theory are largely to blame, I believe, for the insensitive literary judgments by many critics who in other matters are very brilliant, and they are to blame also for a fair amount of bad academic work in literature. At Stanford University, at this writing, we have over one hundred graduate students in English, and about half of these are candidates for the doctorate. We are in a position to select our graduate students very carefully. We accept none who have not made excellent records here or elsewhere, and although some come to us from the smaller institutions (and incidentally some of our best), many come from places like Yale, Harvard, Chicago, Columbia, Princeton, and the better state universities. These people have made excellent records in the past, and most of them make excellent records here; yet almost none can read a line of poetry aloud so that one can discern the structure, and very few can mark the scansion from a line of Shakespeare's sonnets. These people are in these respects the products of their teaching, and the teaching should be improved. Most of our best critics and many of our best-known poets are not much better off. We have sunk into amateurism; and as a result we have in our time the meters of Eliot and of his imitators at the fifth remove, instead of meters comparable to those of the Elizabethans. And we have, worse still, a coherent (and fairly vocal) body of readers so ignorant that they prefer the incompetent to the expert.

If you answer that there are different kinds of poetry and hence we have different kinds of reading (this, of course, is the genteel answer which points to my lack of gentility), I am bound to reply that you are right: there are inferior kinds of poetry. By "inferior," I mean inferior in quality, not smaller in scope. The kind of reading which I defend is equally appropriate to a song by Campion or to an epic by Milton. Any poem which cannot endure the impersonal illumination of such a reading or which requires the assistance, whether expert or clumsy, of shouting, whispering, or other dramatic improvement, is to that extent bad poetry, though it may or may not be a good scenario for a vaudeville performance.

There will never be a first-rate poet or a first-rate critic who lacks a first-rate ear; and no one will ever acquire a first-rate ear without working for it and in the proper manner. Poetry, alas, like painting and music, is an art—it is not a form of happy self-indulgence; and to master an art or even understand it, one has to labor with all of one's mind and with at least a part of one's body.

FOOTNOTES

[1]*Extracts from "A Discourse on the Declamation of Verse,"* by Paul Valéry, translated by Louise Varese. *Paul Valéry, Selected Writings,* New Directions, 1950.

[2]The Influence of Meter on Poetic Convention, in *Primitivism and Decadence,* the essay on John Crowe Ransom, Section IX, in *The Anatomy of Nonsense,* both reprinted in *In Defense of Reason.*

The Poetry

of

Gerard Manley Hopkins

I.

It is my intention to begin by comparing three poems, a sonnet by John Donne, a short poem by Robert Bridges, and a sonnet by Gerard Hopkins, and to compare them with reference to a particular theory of poetry. The poems by Donne and Bridges conform to this theory and illustrate it perfectly; the poem by Hopkins deviates sharply and I believe suffers as a result. Hopkins provides an excellent example of deviation, however, for two reasons: in the first place, though his deviation is serious, it is not crude or ridiculous and thus differs from the deviations of many romantic poets before and after, even poets of genius; and in the second place, his gift for language, as far as his procedure will allow it to emerge, appears almost as great as that of Donne or Bridges, so that we may examine with a minimum of distraction the consequences of the deviation itself. The poems of Donne and Bridges deal with closely related themes, under different figures derived from different views of human history; the theme of Hopkins may be similar but is inadequately defined and one cannot be sure.

The theory of poetry may be summarized briefly as follows. A poem is a statement in words, and about a human experience, and it will be successful in so far as it realizes the possibilities of that kind of statement. This sentence may seem childishly obvious, but it states facts of which we must never lose sight if we are to understand poetry, and facts of which sight is very commonly lost. When we are discussing poetry, we should not beguile ourselves with analogies drawn from music, sculpture, architecture, or engineering; a poem is not a symphony, neither is it a structure made of bricks. Words are primarily conceptual: the words *grief, tree, poetry, God,* represent concepts; they may communicate some feeling and remembered sensory impression as well, and they may be made to communicate a great deal of these, but they will do it by virtue of their conceptual identity, and in so far as this identity is impaired they will communicate less of these and communicate them with less force and precision. It is the business of the poet, then, to make a statement in words about an experience; the statement must be in some sense and in a fair measure acceptable rationally; and the feeling communicated should be proper to the rational understanding of the experience.

Poetry has something, however, though relatively little, in common with music; namely, rhythm. Rhythm, with the other elements of sound which may be combined with it—in poetry these other elements are relatively few and simple—is to some extent expressive of emotion, and it may be used to modify the emotional content of language. The value of rhythm is not primarily in its power to intensify emotion, though it has this power; it is rather in its power to modulate and define emotion, so that a finer adjustment of emotion to thought may be possible.

The poem thus differs from the statement of the philosopher or scientist in that it is a fairly complete judgment of an experience: it is not merely a rational statement, but it communicates as well the feeling which the particular rational understanding ought to motivate. It differs from the statement of the writer of imaginative prose, in that the poet's language is more precise and more flexible and hence can accomplish more in little space and accomplish it better. But with the development of romantic theory in the eighteenth, nineteenth, and twentieth centuries, there has been an increasing tendency to suppress the rational in poetry and as far as may be to isolate the emotional. This tendency makes at best for an incomplete poetry and makes at worst for a very confused poetry.

My first poem is by John Donne:

> Thou hast made me, and shall thy work decay?
> Repair me now, for now mine end doth haste,
> I run to death, and death meets me as fast,
> And all my pleasures are like yesterday;
> I dare not move my dim eyes any way,
> Despair behind and death before doth cast
> Such terror, and my feeble flesh doth waste
> By sin in it, which it toward hell doth weigh;

Only thou art above, and when toward thee
By thy leave I can look, I rise again;
But our old subtle foe so tempteth me,
That not one hour myself I can sustain;
Thy Grace may wing me to prevent his art,
And thou like Adamánt draw mine iron heart.

This poem is simple in conception: the poet looks forward a little
way to death and backward on the sins of his life; he is oppressed
with his helplessness and prays for God's grace that he may love
God, repent, and be saved. The situation is a general one: we
have an orthodox theological definition of a predicament in which
every man is supposed to share; yet the poet knows it to be his
own predicament, and the theological proposition becomes a personal experience. The language is plain, but is exact and powerful.

My second poem, *Low Barometer*, is by Robert Bridges:

The southwind strengthens to a gale,
Across the moon the clouds fly fast,
The house is smitten as with a flail,
The chimney shudders to the blast.

On such a night, when Air has loosed
Its guardian grasp on blood and brain,
Old terrors then of god or ghost
Creep from their caves to life again;

And Reason kens he herits in
A haunted house. Tenants unknown
Assert their squalid lease of sin
With earlier title than his own.

Unbodied presences, the pack'd
Pollution and Remorse of Time,
Slipped from oblivion reënact
The horrors of unhoused crime.

Some men would quell the thing with prayer
Whose sightless footsteps pad the floor,

Whose fearful trespass mounts the stair
Or bursts the lock'd forbidden door.

Some have seen corpses long interr'd
Escape from hallowing control,
Pale charnel forms—nay ev'n have heard
The shrilling of a troubled soul,

That wanders till the dawn hath cross'd
The dolorous dark, or Earth hath wound
Closer her storm-spredd cloke, and thrust
The baleful phantoms underground.

The theme of this poem, as I have said, is similar to the theme
of the sonnet by Donne. Donne sees man as fallen from Grace and
evicted from paradise, and as capable of salvation only through
a return of Grace as an aid to his own imperfect ability; though
he does not say so in this poem, his system depends in part on the
right use of Reason, though Reason without Grace is insufficient,
and the poem is a prayer for Grace. Bridges sees man as risen
from brutality and as governed precariously by Reason. Both
poets deal with man's unequal struggle with his lower nature, and
with what we may call either literally or figuratively the effect of
Original Sin. Bridges, like Donne, feels the need for supernatural
aid in addition to Reason; unlike Donne, he cannot state this
need directly and in theological language, for he is not a Christian, but he implies it in his figurative use of Air: ". . . when Air
has loosed/ Its guardian grasp on blood and brain." Through the
figure of the storm, he indicates supernatural violence; as a result
of the storm, the steady force of the air, like the pressure of water
on submarine life, is relaxed, and man's nature is unbalanced, and
man sees corpses "Escape from hallowing control"; Reason is
overwhelmed by the ancient and powerful demonic forces in its
fleshly habitation. This poem, like Donne's, deals with a common
predicament; unlike Donne's, the poem does not profess to deal
with a personal experience. Both poems deal with the experience
in the most general of terms: Donne's despair, death, and sin
could hardly be more general, but they are definite, for they have

a body of theology behind them, and we know what they include and why Donne feels as he does; Bridges, without such a theological system for direct reference, must limit his statement further:

> Unbodied presences, the pack'd
> Pollution and Remorse of Time,
> Slipped from oblivion reënact
> The horrors of unhoused crime.

These lines are the culmination of his account of sin as the subhuman, the archaic, and the chaotic; he is forced to greater particularity here than Donne, and he achieves greater power, but the statement is nevertheless general and very inclusive. What I wish to call to the attention at present is this: that though both poems are generalized, they are precise; that there is a great difference between generalization and uncertainty.

Let us now consider the sonnet by Hopkins:

> No worst, there is none. Pitched past pitch of grief,
> More pangs will, schooled at forepangs, wilder wring.
> Comforter, where, where is your comforting?
> Mary, mother of us, where is your relief?
> My cries heave, herds-long; huddle in a main, a chief
> Woe, world-sorrow; on an age-old anvil wince and sing—
> Then lull, then leave off. Fury had shrieked 'No lingering! Let me be fell: force I must be brief.'
>
> O the mind, mind has mountains: cliffs of fall
> Frightful, sheer, no-man-fathomed. Hold them cheap
> May who ne'er hung there. Nor does long our small
> Durance deal with that steep or deep. Here! creep,
> Wretch, under a comfort serves in a whirlwind: all
> Life death does end and each day dies with sleep.

This poem differs from the two preceding in that it deals primarily with a particular and personal experience; the difficulty consists in the fact that there is so little generalization that we can feel no certainty regarding the nature of the experience beyond the fact that it has generated a desperate emotion. This is not a poem about the effects of violent emotion in general; it is a poem about a particular violent emotion experienced by the poet. The nearest thing to a statement of motive occurs in the first line and a half of the sestet; but what are these mountains of the mind? One does not enquire because one holds them cheap, but because one has hung on so many oneself, so various in their respective terrors, that one is perplexed to assign a particular motive. One is inclined to ask: "What do you know of these matters? Why are you so secretive? And above all, why are you so self-righteous in your secretiveness?" Hopkins' modern admirers have often assumed that the poem deals with a struggle to maintain what they consider an irrational and unwholesome faith, that it deals with the self-inflicted torture of the religious. There is nothing in the poem either to prove or to disprove the idea of such a struggle. The emotion might result from such a struggle, might result as in Donne's sonnet from a sense of sin either general or particular or both and for the need of Grace, from the contemplation of any of several metaphysical propositions, from the death of a friend, from betrayal by a friend, from the desperation of personal loneliness, from a mixture of some of these, or from something else. We have passed beyond the limits of generalization; we are in the realm of uncertainty; and the mind cannot organize itself to share Hopkins' experience with any real feeling of security.

It is interesting to observe the manner in which he achieves a part of the precision he needs, a small part which is managed with such skill that it gives a brief illusion of a great part, in the use of metaphor. Take, for example, his most brilliant phrase: "on an age-old anvil wince and sing—." The anvil is presumably God's discipline, and on it lies the poet as a piece of metal. The two verbs, the first with its sense of human suffering combined with metallic vibration, the second with its sense of metallic vibration combined perhaps with human triumph, make the metal suffer as metal under the hammer, and the suffering metal is terribly vivid. We suffer with the metal under the blow, and we forget that the literal metal does not suffer, that metal and blow are figurative, and that the human half of the figure is incomplete. Thus the poet conveys emotion for a moment, and conveys it with an illusion of motivation but with no real motivation. If the mountains of the mind were adequately identified, Hopkins' figure would have a power comparable to that of Donne's last line; but Donne's line has meaning, and Hopkins' figure the illusion of meaning.

The meter of the poem contributes to the difficulty, or at least emphasizes it. Hopkins' published explanation of his meter is incomplete and contradictory, and will help us only a little to understand his work. I will consider it in some detail presently, but for the moment I would like to give my own definition of sprung rhythm, which agrees only in part with that of Hopkins, and then proceed to an examination of the meter of the present sonnet. Sprung rhythm occurs when two stresses come together by means other than the normal inversion of a foot; it occurs freely in accentual meter and in syllabic meter; it may occur as a variant in standard English meter as a result of the dropping of an unaccented syllable with the resultant creation of a monosyllabic foot, or as a result of the equally heavy accentuation of both syllables of a foot. For example, when Barnabe Googe writes in an iambic pentameter poem: "Fair face show friends when riches do abound," the first two feet are sprung. It is most profitable, I think, to approach the sonnet under consideration as a variant on iambic pentameter, using Hopkins' remarks as occasional guides. I shall offer a scansion of the poem, with alternative readings of certain lines, and shall then comment on the scansion:

1. No worst/ there is/ none. Pitched/ past pitch/ of grief/,

   No worst/

2. More pangs/ will, schooled/ at fore/pangs wild/er wring/.

3. Comfort/er where/ where is/ your com/forting/?

4. Mary/, mother/ of us/ where is/ your relief/?

5. My cries/ heave, herds/-long; hud/dle in a main/, a chief/

   (My) cries heave/ herds-long/; huddle/ in a main/, a chief/

109

6. Wóe, wórld sór/(row); on an áge/-old án/vil wínce/ and síng/—

   Wóe, wórld sór/row; on an áge/-

7. Then lúll/, then leáve/ off. Fú/ry had shríeked/ 'No líng/-

8. eríng/! Lét me/ be féll/: fórce I/ must be bríef/.'

9. O the mínd/, mínd/ has móunt/ains: clíffs/ of fáll/

10. Fríghtful/, sheér/, nó-man-fáth/omed. Hóld/ them cheáp/

11. Máy who/ ne'er húng/ there. Nór/ does lóng/ our smáll/

    Máy who ne'er/ húng there/. Nór does/ lóng/ our smáll/

12. Dúrance/ deál with/ that steép/ or deép/. Hére! Creép/,

13. Wrétch, un/der a cóm/fort sérves/ in a whírl/wind: áll/

14. Life deáth/ does énd/ and eách/ day díes/ with sleép/.

The first line is normal, unless we read the first foot as reversed; in either version it defines the pattern. In the second line, the first two feet are reversed, and the last three are normal; the reversal of the second foot is unusual, as Hopkins says in his preface, and is the first indication of the violence to follow. In the third line the first and third feet are reversed and the rest normal, this being a more ordinary arrangement. The fourth line is composed of four reversed feet and a normal trisyllabic foot, the first four feet giving us what Hopkins calls counterpoint, or a heard rhythm running counter to the remembered norm. The fifth line may be scanned in either of two ways: as composed of four iambic feet (the first three and the fifth), with the fourth foot reduced to three syllables by the elision of *huddle* and *in;* or with *My* regarded as extra-metrical, a violent procedure from the standpoint of the ordinary metrist, but defensible in Hopkins's system of lines which are "rove over," and thereafter three reversed feet, a normal trisyllabic foot, and a normal dissyllabic. The two readings may be regarded as a case of counterpoint, perhaps, the first giving the theoretic norm and the second the heard rhythm. In regard to this and other elisions, real or possible, in Hopkins, one may suggest that Hopkins may have had a notion comparable to that of Bridges, whereby elision takes place for the eye and so pays its respects to regularity but does not take place for the ear: his elisions, or possible elisions, in any event, are usually preferable if seen but not heard. The sixth line contains seven inescapable accents, and so eliminates any possibility that the poem be scanned as regular accentual meter. I should be inclined to call the first three syllables, all of which are accented, a single sprung foot, of the same sort employed by Googe in dissyllabic units when he wrote, "Fair face show friends." I am acquainted with no poet save Hopkins who has used a sprung foot of three syllables, but the sprung foot of two syllables, employed as a variation on stand-ard English meter, is fairly common in the sixteenth century. The second syllable of *sorrow* may then be regarded as extrametrical, the position of the extra-metrical syllable before the caesura in-stead of at the line-end being natural enough in a system in which the line-end need not involve a pause and in which the caesural break may be heavy, that is in a system of lines which are "rove over," as I have said; or *sorrow* may be elided with *on;* thereafter we have a normal trisyllabic foot followed by three normal dis-syllabics. The seventh line is simple except for the termination in mid-word, a procedure justified by Hopkins' theory and suc-cessful use of "rove-over" rhythm, and for which classical—and even, in a measure, Miltonic—precedent can be found if it is wanted; the fourth foot of this line is a normal trisyllabic, the others are normal dissyllabics. The eighth line contains an in-verted foot in the difficult second position and another in the fourth, and for the rest contains two normal dissyllabics and a final normal trisyllabic, and thus brings the octet back more or less ob-viously to the iambic pentameter pattern.

In the ninth line, we have a trisyllabic, a monosyllabic, and three dissyllabics, the accents falling normally. The monosyllabic foot, as a method of achieving sprung rhythm, has, like the sprung dissyllabic, its precedents in the sixteenth century. It occurs in some of the seven-syllable couplets of Greene: the reader may examine specimens of both, if he is curious, in *The Oxford Book of Sixteenth Century Verse*. In line ten we have an inverted dissyllabic, a monosyllabic, an inverted trisyllabic, and two normal dissyllabics. In the eleventh line we may read five dissyllabics, the first only being inverted; or we may read an inverted trisyllabic followed by two inverted dissyllabics, a monosyllabic, and a normal dissyllabic; the first reading giving the theoretic norm and the second the heard rhythm, with another example of Hopkins' counterpoint as the result. The twelfth line consists of two inverted dissyllabics, a sprung dissyllabic, a normal dissyllabic, and a sprung dissyllabic, to give us another line of seven accents. The thirteenth line consists of an inverted dissyllabic, a normal trisyllabic, a normal dissyllabic, a normal trisyllabic, and a normal dissyllabic. The last line consists of five normal dissyllabics, although the long syllables in the first and fourth feet almost give the illusion of sprung feet: this line returns to the original pattern, yet echoes some of the more violent variations.

The poem, then, is not written in syllabic meter, for the number of syllables varies from line to line; if it is an attempt at accentual meter, it is irregular, for two lines contain extra accents. But it can be described, and without undue trouble, as a variant on standard English meter, a variant both learned and perverse but in which the rhythm is successfully maintained, in which the perversity is equalled by the skill.

Skill to what purpose, however? The rhythm is fascinating in itself, but it does not exist in itself, it exists in the poem. It is a rhythm based on the principle of violent struggle with its governing measure, and it contributes to the violence of feeling in the total poem. But it is this very violence which makes us question the motive, and I think one may add that the violence is in some degree the result of the inadequacy of the motive. When Bridges writes:

> Unbodied presences, the pack'd
> Pollution and Remorse of Time,
> Slipped from oblivion reënact
> The horrors of unhouseled crime,

he is making a statement about human nature which is true and important; the concept and all its implications are clear; and he can make his statement quietly, for he knows that we should recognize its importance and be moved appropriately. I do not mean that the importance of the concept absolves him from the necessity of deliberately communicating the appropriate emotion, and in this passage the emotional weight of the language is great; I mean that his statement has the dignity of conviction. Hopkins has no such generating concept, or at least offers none; since he cannot move us by telling us why he himself is moved, he must try to move us by belaboring his emotion. He says, in effect: "Share my fearful emotion, for the human mind is subject to fearful emotions." But why should we wish to share an emotion so ill sponsored? Nothing could be more rash. We cannot avoid sharing a part of it, for Hopkins has both skill and genius; but we cannot avoid being confused by the experience and suspecting in it a fine shade of the ludicrous. Who is this man to lead us so far and blindfold into violence? This kind of thing is a violation of our integrity; it is somewhat beneath the dignity of man.

II.

I have already indicated the most important general problem raised by Hopkins' meter, the problem of emotional over-emphasis. My actual scansion of the poem in question, however, is one of which Hopkins might or might not have approved, although I suspect that he would have accepted it as reasonable. Before we can deal with Hopkins' meter in general, or at least with reference to his more curious and experimental structures, we must look at his own remarks, for the more difficult poems certainly cannot be scanned as variants on the iambic structure. There are two important documents: *Rhythm and Other Structural Parts of Rhetoric—Verse,* in *The Notebooks and Papers of Gerard Manley Hopkins,* a discussion which is merely a general survey of his speculations on the topic but which gives a fair idea of

113

where his mind had roamed and paused, and the *Author's Preface* to the *Poems,* which was written as an explanation of his actual practice. The former document is only of incidental, though sometimes of real, interest: for example, in my own scansion of the sonnet which I have already discussed, I have indicated a foot of three accented syllables at the beginning of line six, and have noted that this resembles similar feet of two accented syllables which one can find in such Renaissance models as Googe and Nashe, but outdoes them; but Hopkins in the document mentioned lists the Greek *molossus,* or foot of three long syllables, among the various Greek constructions, and since he was aware that English feet resembled certain Greek feet if accent were substituted for length, and since he was all but obsessed with metrical theories of every kind, it is not unreasonable to suppose that he would attempt an English molossus if he were employing a metrical scheme which would at once sustain it and make it recognizable.[1]

The *Author's Preface,* however, was written as an explanation of what Hopkins had actually done. It is unsatisfactory, but we must examine it briefly and point by point. Hopkins begins by naming two kinds of meter, Running and Sprung. The former he identifies with standard English meter; the latter he describes farther on. He states that Running meter may be more easily scanned if any unaccented syllable at the beginning of the line be regarded either as carried over from the preceding line or as extrametrical, so that the accent will always fall in the first place in the foot. It seems obvious to me that such a system of scansion would introduce more difficulties than it would eliminate and further that it would disregard the natural genius of English rhythm. In the following paragraph, however, he proceeds to speak of standard English verse as if he had not made this suggestion: his discussion of reversed feet and of counterpoint rhythm rests on a recognition of the reality of iambic and anapestic feet, and he does not account in any way for this sudden change of theory. One does not know, therefore, how he prefers his own poems to be scanned, and one can only use what judgment one has with the individual poem.

He next takes up Sprung Rhythm, and he offers two distinct definitions for it. First, he says: "Sprung Rhythm, as used in this book, is measured by feet of from one to four syllables, regularly, and for particular effects any number of weak or slack syllables may be used. It [he refers here to the individual foot] has one stress, which falls on the only syllable, if there is only one, or, if there are more, then scanning as above, on the first, and so gives rise to four sorts of feet, a monosyllable and the so-called accentual Trochee, Dactyl, and the First Paeon. And there will be four corresponding natural rhythms; but nominally the feet are mixed, and any one may follow any other." He adds that it will be natural in this rhythm for the lines to be *rove over,* "that is for the scanning of each line immediately to take up that of the one before, so that if the first has one or more syllables at its end the other must have so many the less at its beginning." This is partly a description of the way in which his own poems tend to move with little or no pause at the ends of lines, and it is partly a formal necessity, for if each foot is to start with an accented syllable, there must be some way to account for unaccented syllables when they occur at the beginning of a line, and the obvious method is to assign them to the last foot of the line preceding. What we have here, briefly, is a description of ordinary accentual verse, which commonly shall have a maximum of three unaccented syllables between accents, but which may sometimes have more. Near the end of the *Preface,* however, Hopkins remarks of certain old popular rimes and their modification by time, "however these may have been once made in running rhythm, the terminations having dropped off by the change of language, the stresses come together and so the rhythm is sprung." Here it appears that Sprung Rhythm is identified by the juxtaposition of stresses, and that we may have juxtaposition of stresses in meter other than accentual. For clarity of discussion, I shall use the term *Sprung Rhythm,* as I have used it in the past, to refer to rhythm in which two or more stresses come together, except where this occurs in standard English meter through the mere inversion of a foot.

Of Sprung Rhythm (apparently in either sense), Hopkins says: "Two licenses are natural to Sprung Rhythm. The one is rests, as in music; but of this an example is scarcely to be found in this book, unless in the *Echoes,* second line. The other is *hangers* or *outrides,* that is one, two, or three slack syllables added to a foot and not counting in the nominal scanning. They are so called because they seem to hang below the line or ride forward or backward from it in another dimension than the line itself, according to a principle needless to explain here." This comment is characteristic. As to *The Leaden Echo and the Golden Echo,* it is metrically one of the most difficult of Hopkins' poems, and I believe that there is no way of being certain what the pattern is, if there is indeed a fixed one; there is one insurmountable obstacle to certainty in this matter with regard to all the more difficult specimens, an obstacle which I shall presently discuss. And Hopkins himself appears uncertain as to whether there is a "rest" in the second line. As to *hangers* or *outrides,* he finds it needless to explain their principle; and it is hard to see how so many as six unaccented syllables could be attached to an accented syllable without confusion.

Hopkins cites Greene as having practiced Sprung Rhythm. The Sprung Rhythm which Greene practiced, however, can be classified properly as such according to my definition and to Hopkins' second, but not according to Hopkins' first. Greene's Sprung Rhythm occurs as a variant on standard English meter, when he drops an unaccented syllable, thus bringing two accented syllables together. The following passage, for example, comes from a poem written in ordinary couplets of seven-syllable lines:

> Up I start, forth went I,
> With her face to feed mine eye. . . .

Many similar lines can be found in Greene whenever he uses this form. I should judge that Hopkins must have had such lines by Greene in mind when he was writing his *Lines for a Picture of St. Dorothea,* an early version of *For a Picture of St. Dorothea.* I quote the first stanza, with the accents as given in the published text:

> I bear a basket lined with grass.

I am so líght and fáir

Men are amazed to watch me pass

Wíth the basket I bear.

Which in newly drawn green litter

Carries treats of sweet for bitter.

The meter of Hopkins' second line corresponds exactly to the meter of the first line quoted by Greene, and so does the meter of Hopkins' fourth if one reads the stress that is almost forced on the second syllable of *basket* in spite of its not having been indicated. But there is this difference: Greene's meter is based on the natural stress of the language and is plainly evident without artificial help, whereas no one would suspect the intentions of Hopkins if he had not marked the lines. A structure which is based on so willful a deformation of the language is indefensible, and it will often be grotesque, as it is here; yet Hopkins' more elaborate experiments often depend upon deformations equally fantastic, and the more elaborate structures make his intentions all but indecipherable.

The poem called *Spring and Fall* shows similar deformations in a comparably simple meter; and interestingly enough, most of the deformed lines are pleasanter, though less regular, if read in the normal rhythm of the language. The real trouble inherent in such deformation, however, is apparent when we consider some of the more difficult poems. G. F. Lahey, for example,[2] gives a scansion of *The Windhover*, of which I shall offer only the first four lines. I do not know whether Lahey's scansion is merely a personal hypothesis or whether it is based on markings in a Hopkins ms. It does not correspond with the markings copied for me by a friend from one ms. version of the poem. As previously, I shall indicate the feet with cross-bars:

I caught/ this morn/ing morn/ing's min/ion, king/-

dom of daylight's/ dauphin/, dapple-dawn-drawn/

117

$$\text{Fál}\text{con, in his/ rí}\text{ding/}$$

$$\text{Óf the rólling/ lével under/néath him steady/ ái}\text{r and/}$$

$$\text{stríding/}$$

$$\text{Hígh there, how he/ rúng upon the/ réin of a/ wímpling/ wíng/.}$$

Some of the difficulty in this reading can be eliminated if we pay more attention to Hopkins' theory of "rove-over" lines. That is, unless Hopkins is the ultimate authority for this reading, it would be better to put the first accents of lines three and four on *day-light's* and *rolling* respectively, and to consider the unaccented syllables preceding as parts of the last feet of lines one and two. However, the difficulties do not stop there. As nearly as I am able to pronounce the English language, the normal accentuation of these lines would proceed as follows:

$$\text{I cáught this mórning mórning's mínion, kíng-}$$

$$\text{dom of dáylight's dáuphin dápple-dáwn-drawn Fálcon,}$$

$$\text{in his rí}\text{ding}$$

$$\text{Of the rólling lével undernéath him steády áir, and stríding}$$

$$\text{Hígh there, how he rúng upón the réin of a wímpling wíng.}$$

Furthermore, I submit that this reading gives a better rhythm, in spite of the irregularity of meter (five accents in line one, six in two, seven in three, and six in four). On the other hand, if Lahey's version is defensible with regard to such feet as these—*dom* of daylight's, *Of* the rolling, *neath* him steady—then how are we to know that we should not read likewise: *caught* this morning, *morn*ing's minion? The presence of the unaccented syllable at the beginning of the line provides no obstacle, for Hopkins could easily have regarded it as extrametrical; and these deformations are of exactly the same kind as those offered by Lahey and in fact are more conservative than some of Lahey's. If Lahey's reading is authoritative, then Hopkins expects us to change from normal accentuation to deformed accentuation merely at his own whim, and with no kind of warning, and his own markings of certain poems support this theory. Merely as a technical procedure, this is all but impossible; and if one manages to work it out one gets a mispronunciation of the language which renders the poem ludicrous. In the sonnet which I have already scanned according to my own lights, we found a meter which was very unusual, but which was at the same time comprehensible and pronounceable; its deviations from normal English meter, though made in the interests of an obscurely violent emotion, were structurally both learned and controlled. In *The Windhover*, however, the attempt to express violent emotion through violent meter has got out of hand and become merely preposterous. Lahey adds to this confusion when he tells us[3] that *dapple-dawn-drawn Falcon in his* represent "outrides" or "hangers," though according to his own scansion they do not.

The Windhover is characteristic of Hopkins' more difficult metrical experiments, although it is not one of the most difficult. Other poems which exhibit a similarly confused meter are the following: *The Wreck of the Deutschland, The Starlight Night, Duns Scotus's Oxford, Henry Purcell, The Bugler's First Communion, Spelt from Sibyl's Leaves, The Leaden Echo and the Golden Echo, To What Serves Mortal Beauty, The Soldier, Carrion Comfort,* and *That Nature is a Heraclitean Fire.* There is a good deal of difference in the degree of difficulty among these poems, and there are other poems which exhibit the difficulty. Some of the difficult poems, however, may be read with a fairly satisfactory rhythm, though with irregular meter, if Hopkins' theories are forgotten, although this is a melancholy compromise if one assumes that the poet really meant something by his rhythm.

Mr. Harold Whitehall, in one of the most interesting studies of Hopkins' meter which I have read,[4] constructs a theory of his own on the fragmentary basis left by Hopkins. His theory, briefly and incompletely, is that Hopkins, without realizing it, was composing dipodic meter, or meter in double feet, of the sort described by Patmore, but was using this medium so freely and variously that Patmore did not recognize the results when he saw them. Put thus baldly, the theory may seem a trifle innocent, but actually Mr. Whitehall makes a fairly good case. I am not interested, however, either in attacking or in defending his theory, for in explaining his theory he makes the one admission which, in my opinion, renders his theory worthless as a defense of Hopkins' procedure, in spite of the fact that his theory may conceivably offer a true description of the procedure. He says:

> His sprung rhythm must be read as we read the words of a song when we happen to know the tune. If we do not know the tune—and Hopkins never furnishes it—the words may become, and in print frequently do become, a meaningless jumble of syllables.

But the "tune" of a poem is supposed to be constructed from the living material of the language, not imposed upon it arbitrarily, and Mr. Whitehall is here admitting the defect which I have already described, though he scarcely seems to recognize it as a defect.

The double foot is composed of a major stress and a minor stress, and may have one or two unaccented syllables; it may be combined with the monosyllabic foot, especially when this falls in the last position. What one might call the classical form of the double foot is Hopkins' First Paeon, with the major stress on the first syllable and the minor on the third. A word employed by Mr. Whitehall will illustrate it: *Honeysuckle.* I will mark the scansion, on this basis, of two lines employed by Mr. Whitehall, the first from Alfred Noyes, the second from John Masefield, but will employ a simpler marking than his, one which merely indicates the major and minor accents and the feet. The double accent will indicate the major stress, the single accent the minor:

Músic óf the/ stárlíght/ shímmering ón the/ séa.....

Sándalwóod/, cédarwóod, and/ swéet whíte/ wíne....

The double feet in these lines are real: that is, the poets have chosen their words in such a fashion that clearly recognizable

120

light accents follow clearly recognizable heavy, in a rhythmic pattern which is unmistakable. That this is not, however, the basic pattern of English verse, as Patmore (and I should add Mr. Whitehall with him) would seem to think, one may see readily enough from a brief examination of the following lines:

Of Mǎn's/ first dǐs/obë/dience ánd/ the frǖit/

Of thǎt/ forbïïd/den trëe/ whose mör/tal tǎste/

Brought dëath/ ǐnto/ the wörld/ and ǎll/ our wöe/....

If we regard the first syllable of the first line as extrametrical, we may arrange the feet of this line so that they resemble the feet of Masefield and of Noyes, but we shall be forcing the rhythm and ruining the line; the next two lines cannot be so arranged except by the most arbitrary of accentuation, which will render them ludicrous. The principle which is operating in these lines is different, therefore, from that which we found in the lines preceding. For purposes of the measure, only two kinds of syllable are recognized, the accented and the unaccented; the accented is recognized as such only with reference to the other syllable or syllables within its own foot; and different degrees of accent, since they do not affect the measure, can be infinitely variable and thus contribute to a flexible and perceptive rhythm; the poet is not bound to a simple drum-beat, he can write poetry instead of jingles. When Mr. Whitehall states that standard English meter is largely theoretical and does not lend itself to vocal reading, I can only think that he himself knows very little about the reading of verse.

Hopkins, however, is less simple than Noyes and Masefield. I will offer two lines from Hopkins with Whitehall's accentuation:

Ëarnest, éarthless/, ¨equal, attǔneable/, vǎulty, volǔminous/,

stupéndous/

In this line nothing save forewarning of some kind can indicate that the heavy accents are heavier than the light; so long as one regards the language as it really exists, all of the stresses are equal, and their equality is emphasized by the grammatical parallels: the meter as indicated is a pure fiction. Whitehall runs into even greater difficulty with another line from the same poem:

Her/ fónd yellow hórnlight/ wóund to the wést, her/

wíld hollow hóarlight/ húng to the héight/.

The heavy and light accentuation is equally arbitrary here, and there is the additional confusion that the first syllables of *yellow* and *hollow*, which have a legitimate right to light accent marks, cannot be given them. The reader coming to this line with no previous theory except the realization that there were two kinds of accent involved, would inescapably mark these two syllables as light and every one of Mr. Whitehall's accented syllables as heavy.

We may observe the same kind of accentuation in the conclusion of *The Lantern out of Doors*, which I offer as accented by Hopkins himself according to the published text:

Christ minds; Christ's interest, what to avow or amend

There, eýes them, heart wánts, care haúnts, foot

fóllows kínd,

Their ránsom, their réscue, and fírst, fást, last fríend.

In the light of such scansion, it is curious to read this passage in one of Hopkins' letters to Bridges:

Why do I employ sprung rhythm at all? Because it is the nearest to the rhythm of prose, that is the native and natural rhythm of speech, the least forced, the most rhetorical and emphatic of all possible rhythms.

It is even more curious to read the following comment upon this passage by so able a critic as Arthur Mizener:

However much Hopkins crowded a sentence with repetitions, it never lost the cadence of actual speech; the sound of the voice speaking it is always there in the reader's ear to give the poems their incomparable immediacy.[5]

It is this kind of thing which often makes poetry and the criticism of poetry in our day so baffling a study.

What we have in Hopkin's more difficult constructions, then, is a very complex accentual meter, in which the accents are for the most part the irresponsible inventions of the author rather than native elements of the language, and in which in addition we have "hangers" or "outrides," that is, groups of syllables which may or may not seem to the unassisted reader to have the characteristics of feet, and which are not to be counted in the scansion. Unless we have the author's marking to guide us or are willing to accept on faith the marking of some other authority, we commonly have no way of determining the scansion; and when we have such marking (and this is quite as true of Hopkins' own as of any other), we frequently find ourselves forced into deformations of language which are nearly unpronounceable and are often ridiculous. This metrical method, moreover, is devised in the interest of intensifying an emotion which is frequently unmotivated or inadequately motivated within the terms of the poem. It seems to me obvious that the poems so constructed should be regarded as ruins rather than masterpieces, whatever impressive fragments there may be lying loose among them; and furthermore that defensive explanation is quite foolish. Bridges has been repeatedly rebuked for failing to understand what Hopkins was doing. I am inclined to believe that Bridges understood as much as was necessary, and that the real failure was on the part of Hopkins.

III.

There seems to be some agreement to the effect that Hopkins' commonest method of constructing a poem is to describe a landscape or a part of one and then to provide an application which is usually religious. Arthur Mizener, in an essay devoted very largely to this aspect of Hopkins, writes:

The basic structure of Hopkins' lyrics is a description followed by a comment, an application. They are, for all their intensity, poems of reflection, in the best sense of the word rhetorical rather than dramatic. Occasionally he indulged in the kind of naked symbolism by which the lion, for instance, becomes God's strength and conducts himself accordingly, without regard for the natural habits of lions. At best this practice made for the fantastic kind of poetry we associate with Crashaw. . . .[6]

H. M. McLuhan, in an essay in which interpretation is often carried so far from the actual text as to approach pure fantasy, recognizes the same structure, but regards it as an essential property of a certain kind of religious mind:

Hopkins looks at external nature as a Scripture exactly as Philo Judaeus, St. Paul and the Church Fathers had done. . . . Hopkins habitually shifts his gaze from the order and perspectives of nature to the analagous but grander scenery of the moral and intellectual order. . . . Or the book of nature provides parallel passages with the supernatural revelations of Scripture.[7]

McLuhan illustrates these remarks with quotations which I omit. Mizener is perhaps a little apologetic about the method, but is not greatly disturbed by it; McLuhan seems to regard it as a major virtue. Neither appears to discern certain important difficulties inherent in it.

I will try to illustrate certain of these dangers, beginning with some of the more striking examples and proceeding to the milder ones. I will quote the opening lines of a famous sonnet:

> The world is charged with the grandeur of God.
> It will flame out like shining from shook foil;
> It gathers to a greatness, like the ooze of oil
> Crushed. . . .

The first line offers a major concept, in impressive phrasing. Instead of developing the concept, as a concept, however, in the manner of a poet of the Renaissance, Hopkins proceeds to illustrate it with two descriptive figures. In the first of these we are confronted with the kind of ambiguity which occurs so often in Hopkins: if we assume that the second line is grammatically correct, then *foil* is a quantitative word and refers to tin-foil or to gold-leaf, or to something of that nature, and we have what amounts, in effect, to an image of a mad man (or at least of a remarkably eccentric man) brandishing a metal bouquet; if the foil in question, however, is a fencing foil, then the grammar is defective, for the article is omitted.[8] This particular defect is not an uncommon form of poetic license, especially in Hopkins, and Hopkins takes much greater liberties elsewhere; but the image is indeterminate. In the next image there is a curious inaccuracy of natural description: "crushed" (or spilled) oil does not "gather" to a greatness, it spreads; or if Hopkins is referring to the gathering of oil from the crushing of olives, he is not only incomplete but is again inexact in his grammar. Aside from the difficulties just mentioned, which I suppose will appear trivial to many, but which nevertheless seem to me to introduce an element of shoddiness into the style, both of these figures are almost grotesquely trivial as illustrations of the first line; as so often happens, Hopkins is unable to rise to his occasion, and he relies on violent assertiveness and violent rhythm to carry him over his chasms.

The Starlight Night devotes the octet to ecstatic description of a natural scene. In the first line of the sestet, we have the interjection:

Buy then! bid then! — What? — Prayer, patience, alms, vows.

Then we have two more lines of description, and in the last three lines a statement to the effect that the universe described is the home of "Christ and his mother and all his hallows." It is a curious poem. The description is sometimes extremely brilliant and is interesting everywhere save in the sestet. Yet the real theme of the poem is to be found in the first line of the sestet, and nothing is done with it. A devotional poet of the Renaissance, dealing with "prayer, patience, alms, vows," would have had a good deal to say of each and of what each meant in terms of daily life and toward salvation. The reader who wishes to orient himself, might begin by rereading Ben Jonson's *To Heaven*, John Donne's *Thou hast made me*, Greville's *Down in the depth of mine iniquity*, and Herbert's *Church Monuments*. In no other literary period, I think, save our own, would a poet who was both a priest and a genuinely devout man have thought that he had dealt seriously with his love for Christ and his duty toward him by writing an excited description of a landscape: this kind of thing belongs to the nineteenth and twentieth centuries, to the period of self-expression and the abnegation of reason. The impressiveness of the landscape described in this poem provides a more nearly adequate motivation for the feeling asserted than one can find in many other poems similarly constructed: Hopkins' method in general is to employ the landscape as the immediate motive for a feeling which is too great for it, and then to append the perfunctory moral as a kind of theoretic justification. A few additional poems in which this formula occurs more or less obviously are the following: *Spring, The Sea and the Skylark, The Windhover, Pied Beauty, Hurrahing in Harvest,* and *Duns Scotus's Oxford.* One could add to this list, but these will serve for illustration; and I shall discuss only two of these.

Duns Scotus's Oxford offers an octet devoted to a description of the Oxford landscape, with especial reference to the mingling of city and country and the regrettable domination of the city. The sestet then provides the personal reference:

> Yet ah! this air I gather and I release
> He lived on; these weeds and waters, these walls are what
> He haunted who of all men most sways my spirit to peace;
>
> Of realty the rarest veinëd unraveler; a not
> Rivalled insight, be rival Italy or Greece;
> Who fired France for Mary without spot.

This is the climax and the point of the poem, yet it is obviously very weak. We are told that Scotus is the one "who of all men most sways my spirit to peace"; yet we are not told how he does it nor why. We are told that he is "of realty the rarest veinëd unraveler; a not/ Rivalled insight," yet these are empty epithets, and the subject of the poem, properly speaking, is merely mentioned sentimentally and is not defined or developed. It is as if one should say: "This is a magnificent landscape," or "this is a great man," or "this is the most beautiful woman I have ever seen." What we have is a stereotyped assertion, which we are supposed to take seriously, but which we cannot take seriously for lack of definition and perceptual evidence. This is not the method of Donne, or of Herbert. These poets discuss the subject and omit or pass lightly over the incidentals. Hopkins all but ignores the subject and is at his best in dealing fragmentarily with the incidentals: the "towery city and branchy between towers," and the like. The incidentals are sometimes, as in this line, charming, but they are minor, and they are not incorporated into a well-organized poem, even a minor one, but are parts, rather, of a disorganized poem which pretends to be more than it is.

The Windhover has been named repeatedly as Hopkins' best poem. Hopkins considered it to be such, and his admirers have followed him in this opinion, and some of them have carried it much farther than Hopkins did. McLuhan, for example, says:

> *The Windhover* could never have become the richly complex poem it is if Hopkins had not tested and explored all its themes beforehand, in other poems. There is no other poem of comparable length in English, or perhaps in any language, which surpasses its richness and intensity or realized artistic organization. There are two or three sonnets of Shakespeare . . . which might be put with Donne's "At the round earth's" for comparison and contrast with this sonnet. But they are not comparable with the range of experience and multiplicity of integrated perception which is found in *The Windhover*.[9]

The Windhover begins with the much-discussed description of the bird in flight; if one can keep himself disentangled from perverse theories of scansion while reading it, it is a fine description, but in itself it is merely description, that is, an example of the simplest subject matter available to the poet. As description it can be equalled and even surpassed by a great many passages in Coleridge, Wordsworth, Keats, Hardy, and perhaps others. Hardy's nighthawk, for example, is rendered more clearly and concisely as regards the bird itself; it is free from the pathetic fallacy which occurs in Hopkins' reading of his own ecstacy into an action which for the bird was merely a routine matter of business; and it is not required at any point in the poem to carry a symbolic burden too great for it. I offer Hardy's nighthawk, from the poem entitled *Afterwards*:

> If it be in the dusk when, like an eyelid's soundless blink,
>   The dewfall hawk comes crossing the shades to alight
> Upon the wind-warped upland thorn. . . .

The epithet *dewfall* contributes to the sense of the time of day and suggests the soundless and mysterious appearance of the bird: it does this quite as effectively as Hopkins' *dapple-dawn-drawn* achieves its particular ends, more economically, and perhaps with greater originality. The simile in the first line contributes to both of the same effects. Every detail in the description reinforces every other. There is no vaguely excited and actually inefficient description such as Hopkins' *morning's minion, kingdom of day-light's dauphin.*

The unexplained ecstacy which hangs over the octet is supposedly explained in the sestet:

> Brute beauty and valour and act, oh, air, pride, plume, here
>   Buckle! AND the fire that breaks from thee then, a billion
> Times told lovelier, more dangerous, O my chevalier!
>
> No wonder of it: sheer plod makes plough down sillion
> Shine, and blue-bleak embers, ah my dear,
>   Fall, gall themselves, and gash gold-vermillion.

Before we can discover the degree and kind of success which appear in these lines, however, we must discover the meaning of the words. The first difficulty inheres in the word *buckle;* the second in the identity of the chevalier; and the third in the meaning of the phrase *makes plough down sillion / Shine.*

John Pick, in *Gerard Manley Hopkins, Priest and Poet*, has this to say, after discussing the beauty described in the octet:

> But here is a beauty far, far greater. And the sestet is devoted to a revelation of a beauty beyond this beauty, a beauty which is "a billion times told lovelier, more dangerous" than the purely natural and triumphant flight. And whence comes this achieve-

ment which is more than achievement, this mastery which is more than mastery?

It is in the act of "buckling," when the windhover swoops down, when its flight is crumpled, when "brute beauty and valour and act, oh, air, pride, plume" in an act of self-immolation send off a fire far greater than any natural beauty. . . . Nor is this to be wondered at, for this is true even in humble little things —is true of everything: the sheen of common earth shines out when the plough breaks it into furrows; and fire breaks from fire only in the moment of its own destruction. . . . Here is Christ upon the Cross and Hopkins the *alter Christus*. Beautiful was Christ's public life, but "a billion times told lovelier" was His self-immolation on the Cross, His sacrifice transmuted by the Fire of Love into something far greater than any mere natural beauty. More beautiful than any natural achievement was Hopkins' own humble and plodding continuance of the ethic of redemption through his own mystical self-destruction, his own humble following of Christ to the very Cross of Calvary. And the beauty of Christ and the beauty of the Jesuit to eyes that see more than this world is the beauty of their dying to live.[10]

Pick selects one of several possible meanings for *buckle*: for him the word means to collapse, as if we should say, "The wings of the plane buckled and it crashed." He finds support for his general interpretation in the writings of Loyola, which Hopkins as a Jesuit had studied carefully, and from scattered passages in Hopkins' other writings. But we have no right to suppose that any poem by Hopkins is a gloss on Loyola or on anything else unless there is clear evidence in the text, and there is no such evidence here. The falcon's wings do not buckle, in this sense, when he dives: they are retracted close to the body, or else are raised directly above the body, and are under perfect control; the dive, or the drop, of the falcon is one of the most remarkable physical facts observable in brute nature. Furthermore, the dive or the drop is not an act of self-sacrifice, it is an attack on the bird's prey. If Pick's interpretation is right, then the poem is badly conceived from start to finish; but it would be unfair to Hopkins to read into his poem a meaning for which the poem offers no evidence and which, once it is there, ruins the poem.

Pick apparently takes the expression *O my chevalier!* as being addressed to Christ, but there is no real evidence of this either. Christ is not mentioned in the poem. The poem is dedicated *To Christ our Lord,* but this does not mean that the poem is addressed to Christ. When a man dedicates a novel to a friend, he does not imply that the novel is addressed to his friend or is about him— he is merely offering a gift: since Hopkins regarded this as his best poem, he may merely have offered it to Christ in homage. On the other hand, it is possible that Hopkins meant to imply address in the dedication; there is no way of being sure. The difficulty in the second tercet is a minor one, in the sense that it does not affect the interpretation of the poem, but it is troublesome with respect to the particular image. The question is this: does Hopkins mean to say that the sheer plodding of the plowman makes the plow shine as it goes down the furrow, or does he mean to say that the plowed-down earth is made to shine? If the first meaning is correct, then *plough* is a noun and should have an article; if the second meaning is correct, then *plough* is a past participle incorrectly spelled for the sake of euphony. The first of these licenses, though awkward, is common, not only in Hopkins but in other poets; the second would be violent and unlikely in any other poet, but is plausible enough in Hopkins. Pick believes that the earth shines and not the plow; but the passage has been taken in both ways by various critics.

McLuhan is at least as adventurous as Pick in his departures from the text. He writes:

> To a member of a militant order whose founder was a Spanish soldier or chevalier, the feudal character of the opening imagery is quite natural. "Minion," "dauphin," "valour," "plume," and "buckle" alike evoke the world of dedicated knighthood and shining panoply of armor. Thus the mounted chevalier flashing off exploit as he "rung upon the rein" enables Hopkins later to reverse the situation with great dramatic effect in "sheer plod makes plough down sillion Shine." The paradox consists in the fact that Hopkins as lowly plowman following a horse flashes off infinitely more exploit than Hopkins the imagined chevalier.

More central still to the dramatic movement is the way in

which the chevalier images of the octet are concentrated in "here Buckle!" Buckling is the traditional gesture of the knight preparing his armor for action. A buckler is the bright shield of defense bearing insignia, flashing defiance . . . I have already said that "here" means in the "obedient and humble heart" and that "Buckle" means that the "brute beauty" of the bird as the mirror of God's grandeur is to be transferred or flashed to the "heart in hiding," just as the burnished surface of the plow in action is hidden in the earth. The high-spirited but obedient heart of man is "a billion times" better a mirror of Christ the chevalier than is the mirror of the external world. . . .[11]

McLuhan supports his interpretation at some length by quoting passages from other poems which suggest the theme which he has here in mind; my objection to his interpretation is simply that he departs too appallingly far from the actual text of the poem in hand. It is worth noting in passing that he agrees with Pick in the meaning of *chevalier,* and that, although he seems here to accept the other meaning of the plow image, he yet accepts both meanings of this latter in the course of his essay.

Miss Ruggles, although she believes that the plow shines rather than the earth, offers a more direct and simple explanation of the other phrases, and she gives us an interpretation which we can find justified, more or less, in the text. She says:

His imagination is caught and lifted as the small spiralling creature, magnificent in his instinctive performance, hovers at the very crux of its mastery, poised almost stationary against the opposing tide of wind.

Brute beauty and valour and act, oh, air, pride, plume, here Buckle!

This is the ultimate assertion, the carrying out of selfhood—

AND the fire that breaks from thee then, a billion Times told lovelier, more dangerous, O my chevalier!

It is in the act of buckling, when every sinew and chord of the identity thrills, at grips with its appointed function, that the beauty of the self flares brightest.

131

> No wonder of it: shéer plód makes plough down sillion
> Shine, and blue-bleak embers, ah my dear,
>   Fall, gall themselves, and gash gold-vermilion.

The crude plough gleams in the moment of its contact with the resistful soil. Embers, foredoomed to crumble, can glow in this obscure enactment as fiercely as the flame.[12]

Miss Ruggles interprets the poem in terms of the concept of haecceity, inscape, or selfhood, which so obsesses Hopkins, and so keeps the poem closer to the bird which it apparently describes. For her, *buckle* means to concentrate all one's powers, as when we say: "He buckled to his work." And for her, the chevalier is the bird itself. She, also, is able to support her interpretation through other passages in Hopkins. In terms of her interpretation, we have a conclusion in the second tercet which merely points out that much less impressive actions give off their own fire: the first, the plodding effort of the plowman, which is humble but active; the second, the passive action of the coals when they fall and light up; so that it is no wonder that the striking action of the bird should give off a superior fire.

With this interpretation in mind, we may return to McLuhan for a moment. McLuhan assumes that Hopkins is developing a single chivalric image until he gets to the last tercet and abandons it, but the skate image interrupts this, and even McLuhan makes no effort to translate it into chivalric terms; it is the usual procedure of Hopkins, moreover, to hurl miscellaneous images at his subject from all sides, rather than to develop one of them fully. There is no reason to accept McLuhan's interpretation of *buckle,* therefore, unless it draws the whole poem together, which it fails to do. McLuhan believes that the plowman is figuratively Hopkins, but the poem does not say so; McLuhan says that the figurative plowman "flashes off infinitely more exploit than Hopkins the imagined chevalier," but the poem says that it is no wonder that the bird at the height of his achievement should flash light when a mere plowman can do it in a small way. McLuhan says that "here" means "in the obedient and humble heart," but Hopkins says nothing about obedience and humility, and of his heart he says "my heart in hiding," which on the face of it seems to mean "my heart within me," or "my heart unobserved."

Miss Ruggles takes another step in her interpretation, which brings her closer to Pick and to McLuhan, though still leaves her far behind them. She says:

> The beauty and valor of the winging falcon are Christ's own beauty and valor in an unthinking and finite form. Thus in a sense, the windhover is Christ. Christ is the windhover.

The poem does not say this, and the dedication does not necessarily imply it, but this interpretation would be in line with Hopkins' thought and with his practice in other poems; it would offer, moreover, some explanation of the violent rhapsody of the first tercet. This brings us to the crucial weakness of the poem, however; for if Miss Ruggles is right at this point, as I suspect she is, then the poem falls short of its theme in just about the same fashion as does the poem on Duns Scotus. To describe a bird, however beautifully, and to imply that Christ is like him but greater, is to do very little toward indicating the greatness of Christ.

Let me illustrate this objection with an account of my own experience. For more than thirty years I have bred and exhibited Airedales in a small way, and I have owned some very fine ones. At the present time I own a young dog who seems to me exceptionally beautiful, especially when he is in motion. No less than Hopkins' falcon, he is one of God's little creatures; he is probably a much better specimen of his kind and better adapted to his peculiar ends, and if one is sufficiently scholarly and sufficiently perceptive, one will be aware of this probability; in addition, I am fairly certain that his moral character is more admirable than that of the bird. Yet it would never occur to me to write a poem describing his beauty and then stating that the beauty of Christ was similar but merely greater. To do so would seem to me ludicrous, and to many it would seem blasphemous. Yet there is no essential difference between my dog and Hopkins' bird; the bird has the advantage merely of the Romantic and sentimental feeling attached to birds as symbols of the free and unrestrained spirit, a feeling derived very largely from Shelley's *Skylark* and from a handful of similar—and similarly bad—poems of the past century and a half. Hopkins' poem employs a mechanical and a very easy formula. His image resembles the image of the anvil in *No worst, there is none,* in which we get the physical embodiment of the meaning, without the meaning, or with too small a part of it. To defend this sort of thing with pretentious remarks about the "sacramental view of nature" is merely foolish, no matter how numerous, pious, and ancient the precedents which one may be in a position to cite.

Even if we leave Christ out of it and confine the poem to the bird, we find much the same difficulty in the first tercet: the light that flashes from the bird when he buckles is "a billion times told lovelier, more dangerous" than it was before; but the degree and kind are the important things, and one is not given them. We are left where we were left with the "rarest-veined unraveller, a not rivalled insight," in *Duns Scotus's Oxford.*

I would like to add one minor suggestion in post-script. I am no great philologist, myself, but in my casual reading of the more obvious dictionaries I have observed that the word *buckle,* in Scots and in northern English, sometimes means *to marry.* In this sense, the word would function as well as it would in any other sense. I am not aware that Hopkins ever made a notation of this meaning of the word, though he may have done so; but we know that Hopkins was inordinately fascinated with folk locutions and examined them endlessly, and this interest strikes me as being quite as relevant to the poem as his training in Loyola or his interest in Duns Scotus's theory of haecceity. What the word actually means in the poem, I confess I do not know. The reader may proceed from this point as he sees fit.

What should the verdict be on such a poem? As I have shown, the metrical intentions of the poet are more than uncertain and are probably unsound; but one can make out fairly well with the rhythm if one simply reads the poem as it seems to be written. The crucial statement of the poem, regardless of the interpretation which one accepts, appears to occur in the second and third lines of the first tercet, yet this statement is merely an *assertion* of importance and of excitement, it is not an explanation and description. The sestet contains three expressions which have led to various interpretations and of which no interpretation is certain. As to *buckle,* Pick's interpretation (like my own as well), has grammar on its side; for if McLuhan is right, the expression should be *buckle on,* and if Miss Ruggles is right, it is *buckle to,* and each of these calls for an object. But grammar is worth very little as a criterion in dealing with Hopkins; he violates grammar as he sees fit, and the interpreter can seldom call it to witness. He violates grammar as he sees fit, mainly to gain results which he considers more valuable than grammar: striking epithets and striking phonic effects. But the phonic effects are frequently over-wrought and badly wrought, and the epithets, when they do not overwhelm the subject with an assortment of ill-adjusted details, are likely to be incomprehensible because of the way in which they have been attained. The first tercet fails to define its subject; the second tercet is more nearly comprehensible, but in itself is not very effective, especially with regard to the embers: the function of the embers in the total theme seems clear enough, at least in Miss Ruggles' terms, but the embers as embers, as "inscape," are described in language which is coarse and imperceptive. The language is violent, and it continues both the tone of strong emotion and the rhythm which seem to have been established, but it offers a poor perception of embers as such. The description of the bird in the octet is impressive in the main, though I believe that it has been over-rated. The bird is apparently used to symbolize the perfection of Christ, but the haecceity of the bird and the haecceity of Christ are very different matters indeed, and of the haecceity of Christ we are told precisely nothing in the poem. Unless Christ is symbolized, however, or unless something far greater than the bird is symbolized, then the ecstatic tone of the poem is not justified; and in fact it is not justified if Christ is symbolized, for it could be justified only by an indication of those qualities of Christ which would serve the purpose. The poem is romantic both in its over-wrought emotionalism and in its carelessness. It is not the greatest sonnet ever written, nor even the best poem in Hopkins; it is a poem of real, but minor and imperfect virtues, and that is all.

What, conceivably, are the reasons for the kind of poetry which we have observed in Hopkins?

As to the biographical reasons, we can merely surmise, and although I confess to some distaste for biographical surmises, which are invariably both inascertainable and in the nature of arguments *ad hominem,* nevertheless certain guesses are hard to lay aside. Whatever the reasons may have been, Hopkins in his later years passed through a period of psychological crisis in which his mental balance, if he really preserved it at all times, was precarious. The reasons for this crisis are hard to guess, and perhaps are not important, but the crisis appears to have been real. There was, however, a trace of effeminacy in Hopkins, which one can see in his portraits, in his letters, and in his poems, which may well have been at least in part the cause of the matter. The conflict between such a weakness or some other weakness and his faith and vocation may at times have been acute, though I suspect that his faith and vocation were his chief source of strength, and not, as some writers have supposed, a source of weakness. Whatever the nature of his difficulty, his struggle with it, so far as we may judge, was desperate, and, in spite of its lack of intellectual clarity, little short of heroic. The difficulty seems to have been real, and Hopkins at the same time did not deal with it intelligibly in his poems, though his poems appear to have been affected by it. There is in a large portion of his verse an element of emotional violence which is neither understood nor controlled.

Historically, Hopkins belongs to the late Romantic period. The text-book dates for the Romantic period (1798 to 1832) are merely an academic convention, designed primarily for the organization of university courses. The Romantic period began, one may reasonably say, in 1711, with the publication of Shaftesbury's *Characteristics;* it reached a succinct identity in the early 1730's, with the publication of Pope's *Essay on Man,* more particularly with the third and fourth Epistles. In spite of contending forces, the Romantic movement has gained steadily in strength to the present time. The movement represents, essentially, a rebellion against the authority of reason in favor of the authority of impulse and emotion. In Pope this was a matter of theory, not of practice: Pope's practice was inherited from an earlier period and from better ideas. By the middle of the eighteenth century, with Gray, Collins, Smart, and others, it was a matter of both theory and practice, and practice has been more and more influenced into our time. In Hopkins' own time, as Arthur Mizener has indicated, Romantic ideas and practice tended to fuse with erudition and with erudite eccentricity, and we meet such figures as Doughty, Carlyle, and Browning, just as we meet in the twentieth century such studious eccentrics as Pound, Eliot, and Marianne Moore. It is not curious, then, that Hopkins should be inclined by his personal nature and by his historical setting about equally to practice an extremely emotional and eccentric form of poetry.

But Hopkins was a Catholic priest, and Catholic doctrine exalts reason, teaches distrust of impulse, and insists on a measure of conformity to familiar norms. That his faith and his vocation disciplined Hopkins' personal life I believe to be undeniable, in spite of such eccentricities as he showed: had it not been for the faith and the vocation, the eccentricities might well have been disastrous. But the question arises as to what interpretation of Catholic doctrine he found which justified him in writing poetry of the kind in which he commonly indulged himself. The answer to the question is not far to seek.

Among the *Fragments, Etc.* published at the end of the *Poems of Gerard Manley Hopkins* is a poem entitled *On a Piece of Music*.[13] Of this poem John Pick writes as follows:

> But as we approach the study of the poems which Hopkins wrote, we come to the judgment of the work of art and we must be careful not to praise it for the wrong things. Its religious significance does not in itself give it poetic greatness; it may express a sacramental view of nature, and yet it may be an inferior poem. Whether it is art or not depends on artistic standards. "The standard and aim is strict beauty," Hopkins wrote to Bridges, "and if the writer misses that his verse, whatever its incidental merits, is not strict or proper poetry." Hopkins expressed this

in another way in saying that a work of art is "good" or less good, but as such is not right or wrong:

> Therefore this masterhood,
> This piece of perfect song,
> This fault-not-found-with good
> Is neither right nor wrong. . . .
>
> No more than Re and Mi,
> Or sweet the golden glue
> That's built for by the bee.

The poem from which these lines are taken, "On a Piece of Music" (an undated fragment), makes the important distinction which was maintained by the scholastic tradition—the distinction between art and prudence. Maritain has carefully shown the importance of differentiating between the two, and here we can but follow his analysis. While art operates "ad bonum operis," for the good of the work done, prudence operates "ad bonum operantis," for the good of the worker. Art as such has no other end than the perfection of the work made, and not the perfection of the man making. That is the view that Hopkins also supported.

But in the same poem the Jesuit wrote:

> What makes the man and what
> The man within that makes:
> Ask whom he serves or not
> Serves and what side he takes.
>
> For good grows wild and wide,
> Has shades, is nowhere none;
> But right must seek a side,
> And choose for chieftain one.

In these lines he is concerned not with the work of art as such, but with the artist; not with the end of art, but with the end of man; not with art but with prudence.

While art concerns a local end, says St. Thomas, prudence concerns the whole of human life and its last end. Thus while "the sole end of art is the work itself and its beauty. . . . for the man making, the work to be done comes into the line of morality and so is merely a means." The end of the work of art is beauty but the end of man is God. "If the artist," according to this view, "were to take for the final end of his activity, that is to say for beatitude, the end of his art or the beauty of his work, he would be, purely and simply, an idolator."

All poets may be—and ultimately must be—judged from both points of view. The great devotional poet must be at the same time a great poet and a deeply religious man.

It will readily be observed that this view of art differs radically from the view which I myself am defending. According to my own view, the poem is a rational statement about a human experience, made in such a way that the emotion which ought to be motivated by that rational understanding of the experience is communicated simultaneously with the rational understanding: the poem is thus a complete judgment of the experience, a judgment both rational and emotional. The poetic medium is simply a means to a finer and more comprehensive act of understanding than we can accomplish without it. The poem thus falls under the heading of prudence, to continue with the scholastic terms; it is a method for perfecting the understanding and moral discrimination; it is not an obscurely isolated end in itself. I believe that my own view of art is more Thomistic than the one which Pick offers, that it is more in conformity with Thomistic philosophy as a whole; for it relates a major human activity to the whole of human life, to the economy of redemption, so to speak, and does not leave it dangling. On the other hand, Thomas is largely to blame, I suspect, for this construction of what he wrote of art. He apparently did not take the arts seriously enough to treat them systematically. At any rate, he did not treat them in the systematic fashion in which he treated almost everything else, but merely used such ideas of art as he possessed to illustrate other matters, so that the person seeking his views on the subject must search for many brief and scattered comments and relate them as best he can. There are passages among these comments which make the interpretation offered by Pick appear doubtful, but there are others which support it; and nowhere that I can discover is there a clear statement of the relationship of the form to the subject, a statement that will bring the form demonstrably within the moral order and the order of understanding. Thomas is guilty of one confusion, for example, which is common among estheticians: he appears to find a common quality in what we call the beauty of nature and in what we call the beauty of art. A beautiful natural object, however, is not in itself an act of human judgment; it is outside of the moral order. And although a man's apprehension of such an object, and evaluation of it, is an act of judgment and within the moral order, this apprehension and evaluation can occur only in an act of criticism or in a descriptive work of art. If the artist, however, is conceived as one who creates objects comparable to natural objects, he is working outside of the moral order, and this notion will result in one form or another of a doctrine of art for art's sake, of art "ad bonum operis." From my own point of view, the natural object cannot be viewed as a work of art, for it is not a work of human judgment; but as a part of human experience, and like any other part of human experience, it is a legitimate subject for art.

It is not my purpose, at present, however, either to attack Thomas or to defend him. Regardless of whether Thomas may be held responsible for the opinions which Pick summarizes, a good many students of Thomas have derived them, and what concerns me at the moment is the fact that Hopkins is among these.

As Pick indicates, however, there is a moral rider. The poet *as a man* has moral responsibilities; he should if possible encourage virtue, and above all he should not encourage vice. But in regard to this function, he will operate, presumably, in the way of choosing his subject—there is no idea that morality of any kind is involved in the treatment of the subject. What we have is a kind of ecclesiastical version of the Horatian compromise, with much leeway on the one hand for a barbarous moral criticism, and great freedom on the other for stylistic irresponsibility on the part of the poet. In *The Notebooks and Papers of Gerard Manley Hopkins* there is an early composition entitled *On the Origin of Beauty: A Platonic Dialogue,* which begins by deriving the principles of beauty from natural objects, and which concludes by discussing poetic beauty wholly in terms of construction, and which establishes no relationship between form and subject, which establishes, in other words, form as a thing and an end in itself. On the other hand, we may find the ethical criterion in a letter to Baillie in 1868:

> I cannot find yr. letter unfortunately or wd. look again about *The Lady with the Camellias*. I remember however that you assume I shall contradict whatever you say. I dare say it is a graceful and pathetic story—why shd. it not be? With regard to the morality it is true no doubt [absolutely] that any subject may be chosen for its art value alone and so will not, or rather need not, be any scandal to the writer or reader. The question, however, is the practical effect, and is of course one of degree, where no line can be drawn. I mean for instance that it is impossible not personally to form an opinion against the morality of a writer like Swinburne, where the proportion of these subjects to the whole is great and secondly where the things themselves are the extreme cases in their own kind. Another thing is, that what is innocent in a writer, if it must cause certain scandal to readers becomes wrong on that ground. This too is a question of degree for perhaps we are not bound to consider those who will take scandal from everything: it is required that the number only shd. be small. Then with the work itself the question is how far in point of detail one may safely go—another question of degree: one thinks e.g. Othello shd. be called innocent, Ovid immoral . . .[14]

One observes here that a work may have an *art value alone*, but that it should also deal with an innocent subject, that is, should not be "immoral." But the concept of art is completely divorced from the concept of morality so far as any functional relationship goes. Swinburne is immoral because of the nature of his subjects, not because he falsifies them in the interests of excessive and sentimental decoration. In these terms, Baudelaire would be quite as immoral as Swinburne, because of his subjects, and Hopkins himself would be invariably a moral poet because of his subjects. Yet in my own terms, Baudelaire is at least very often a profoundly moral poet because of his understanding of his subjects, and Hopkins is very often an immoral poet for much the same reasons why Swinburne seems to me immoral. To say that 'Othello is "innocent" strikes me as curious. *Othello* is rather a triumph of the active understanding. To demonstrate the structural proportions of *Othello* on the one hand, and to prove it morally innocuous on the other, will not get us very far on the way to an understanding of its greatness; and yet Hopkins' ideas about literary art will provide him with the tools to do no more than this.

These ideas will justify (within the limits mentioned) a perfectly romantic art: emotional intensity for its own sake, metrical elaboration for its own sake, metaphor for its own sake, repetition and elaboration of structure for their own sakes. The poem becomes at once an unrestrained indulgence in meaningless emotion, and an unrestrained exercise in meaningless ingenuity; the poet has no responsibility to understand and evaluate his subject truly. If one will consider such poems as *The Wreck of the Deutschland, The Loss of the Eurydice, Binsey Poplars, Spelt from Sybil's Leaves,* and *The Leaden Echo and the Golden Echo,* to mention only some of the more obvious examples, one will find the perfect product of the theory. The paraphrasable content of all of these poems is so slight as to be reducible to a sentence or two for each. The structures erected upon these simple bases are so fantastically elaborate that the subjects are all but lost and the poems frequently verge upon the ludicrous.[15]

A more or less recent book on Hopkins inadvertently throws a good deal of light on these matters.[16] The chapters have the following titles: (1) The Meaning of 'Inscape' and 'Instress,' (2) 'Inscape' and Canons of Poetry, (3) Current Language Heightened, (4) Perception and Expression of Inscape, (5) Inscaping the Word. The first of these makes an excellent distinction between Hopkins' conception of *inscape* as the individuating form of an object, and *instress* as the force internal to the object and which maintains that form. The second deals very loosely with Hopkins' somewhat loose critical theories. The remaining chapters deal with various aspects of Hopkins' diction and phrasing. There is no discussion of meter. In connection with diction and phrasing, the author, Peters, sometimes belabors the obvious, and he sometimes ventures on hyperbolic flights into the remoter regions of fantasy, but his analyses are often helpful and his chief value resides in them—provided the reader be reasonably cautious.

Peters forces our attention upon certain of Hopkins' ideas which have perhaps never been adequately considered; the trouble is that he seems to do little more than clarify to a greater or a less degree the concepts which Hopkins had in mind and fails utterly to evaluate them or investigate their relationships to comparable ideas in other fields. Peters points out (what we already knew) that Hopkins was greatly preoccupied with the 'inscapes' of natural objects, mainly with reference to the visual aspects of the objects; he emphasizes (what perhaps we have realized less fully) that Hopkins was also preoccupied with his own 'inscape.' The latter preoccupation is scarcely distinguishable from the Romantic preoccupation with self-expression, and Peters discusses it at length in the jargon of self-expressionism, though neither Hopkins nor Peters appears to be aware of this similarity. When Hopkins discovered Scotus, as Peters points out, he recognized the Scotist doctrine of *haecceitas* as a kind of metaphysical explanation of his perception of inscapes, and was delighted with it. I am not as familiar with Scotus as I no doubt should be, but as I understand the matter, the doctrine of *haecceitas* is merely an attempt to describe in metaphysical terms the observable fact of individuation, and it involves no sentimental preference for the preservation of any given state of individuation. But for Hopkins (and Peters approves of this), as for the Romantics, the soul as it is at any given moment is a thing to be cherished and expressed.

Now as nearly as I can understand this matter, which is a troublesome one, we are concerned with two orders of individuation: the intellectual and the material. Aquinas tells us that God is perfect being and that all creatures are in one way or another and in varying measures imperfect. Aquinas is concerned here with intellectual being. This doctrine is not only orthodox Catholic doctrine, but it is generally accepted Christian doctrine, and Hopkins and Peters, especially as Jesuits, are presumably committed to it. But if this is true doctrine, then intellectual individuation may be defined in terms purely and simply of kinds and degrees of imperfection, and there is nothing in it to be cherished or admired. If we were all perfect, we should all be precisely alike, for in matters of the mind there is only one perfection. We may, of course, assume the perfect mathematical mind, the perfect poetical mind, and so on, but these would not be perfect minds, they would be perfect only in particular and limited departments. There is only one perfection, and it has no degrees: there are degrees only of imperfection. Lest this concept terrify the timid, let me hasten to add that I see little likelihood of this state of universal perfection in any predictable future. So far as their theory of poetry is concerned, however, our two Jesuits appear to have forgotten that we are fallen men; and Peters writes as if Hopkins were one of the "beautiful souls" of Romantic tradition.

In my terms, it is the business of the poet, not to communicate his own inscape, but to arrive at a true judgment of his subject, whatever it may be; we all have individuality, but few of us have intelligence. Peters and Hopkins remind one of the young lady who was studying art under a French master and who protested against his methods, saying: "But I cannot express my personality when I draw as you tell me," and to whom the master replied: "Mademoiselle, no one except mama is interested in your personality." Hopkins is one of a number of Romantics (Poe is another example) who have protested against the lack of originality in English poetry and have set out to do something about it. Yet English poetry is beyond much doubt the greatest single body of literature produced in Europe, at any rate this side of the Greeks; and if originality is not greatly in evidence, perhaps originality is not one of the ingredients of greatness. In point of fact, if one will take Donne's *Thou hast made me,* Greville's *Down in the depth,* Jonson's *To Heaven,* or *Though beauty be the mark of praise,* Herbert's *Church Monuments,* and Bridges' *Low Barometer,* or *Eros,* one will find a minimum of the eccentricities either of the poets or of their periods, and a great and pervasive similarity of tone and of method. These are among the greatest short poems in English, and the list could be very much extended without damage to the conclusions. Such poets are trying to exhibit the truth, they are not trying to exhibit themselves, and they tend to resemble each other.

The individuation of material objects may well be a different matter, at least in many of their aspects. Physically, there is no such thing as the perfect man: there may well be the perfect boxer, the perfect wrestler, the perfect jockey, or the perfect hurdler, but they will be of different types, and many of their physical characteristics will be irrelevant to their functions. If we assume that Joe Louis represents the type of the perfect boxer, nevertheless the color of his skin has no bearing on his perfection: it happens to be brown; it might as well be white, green, or yellow. When we proceed from this type of material form through the lower animals, the plants, and the minerals, the area of irrelevance increases, the curiosities of accidental forms and relationships become more numerous, and the type of person who is fascinated by natural curiosities may find here a legitimate and harmless pasturage provided he knows what he is doing and does not confuse his activities with activities of a different kind.

If, however, we have a poet who is concerned with the expression of his own inscape (self-expression) and with the inscapes of natural objects and with little else, we may expect him to produce poems which are badly organized, and loosely emotional, and which endeavor to express emotions obscure in their origins and to express these emotions in terms of natural details of landscape to which the emotions are irrelevant. And poems of this kind are what Hopkins most often wrote. It is remarkable that not once does Peters analyze a poem from beginning to end. He analyzes passages, lines, phrases, and words; that is, fragments. Hopkins is a poet of fragments for the most part, and it is only if one can enjoy a chaos of details afloat in vague emotion that one can approve the greater part of his work. Peters is invariably a critic of fragments; it appears never to have occurred to him that a poem is more than a conglomeration of details; and hence he never discovers the real trouble with Hopkins.

Peters' concept of the poem as a congeries of suggestions is most obvious in his defense of Hopkins' homophones. In *The Windhover*, for example, Peters informs us that *told* has the additional meaning of *tolled;* that *rung* refers not only to an exercise in horsemanship but refers also to little bells ringing on the reins; that *rein* also means *reign*. At this rate *buckle* might well be accepted in every signification that we can find for it in the NED, but when we have done we shall have a much worse poem than I think Hopkins intended. This kind of thing, whether in theory or in practice, represents one of the ultimate stages of Romantic disintegration: when the Society of Jesus has come to this, the rest of us had better take stock of our ideas.

It is true that Peters cites passages from Hopkins to prove that the poet should deal with truth and exhibit earnestness. But neither Hopkins nor Peters would seem to have any idea of what these terms mean in connection with the making of a poem. The *truth* would seem to be of the kind which I have indicated; the earnestness a confused and violent religious emotion. Two of the most earnest men produced by our civilization were J. J. Rousseau and R. W. Emerson, and both were convinced that they were teaching the truth. It is a pity that the Jesuits, or at least the literary men among them, do not study these two writers along with their Suarez and Loyola; to do so would make better Thomists of them, and would make them sadder and more sober men.

V

What, then, can we salvage from Hopkins? Among the poems with which I have not already dealt in at least some small measure, one should consider the following, I believe, if only tentatively:

The Habit of Perfection is an early poem which has been treated by Hopkins' admirers in a more or less patronizing fashion. The poem contains one phrase to which I should make slight objection: *the hutch of tasty lust*. The word *hutch* is irrelevant to the perception, and the word *lust* forces the perception, and the combination of sounds is difficult. Nevertheless the poem is free from the later excesses, is remarkably well executed, and deals with a serious topic; I should name it as one of the best.

The Valley of the Elwy reverses in a sense Hopkins' commonest formula, that of description and religious application. It begins with the general description of a scene, partly human and partly natural, which Hopkins loved; then, instead of proceeding from natural beauty to the beauty of God, the poem states that the humans are unworthy of the general loveliness of the scene, and the poem ends with a prayer that God grant them his grace. The poem is simple and honest; there is no unarticulated violence—in fact, there is nothing unarticulated and there is no violence; it is not a great poem, but it is moving. The meter contains some of Hopkins' innovations, but in a quiet form.

Andromeda is an unfortunate compromise between the methods of Hopkins and of Milton. The poem is reasoned from beginning to end: the parts are rationally related; one leads to another; there is nothing extraneous. The fable is a good one: Andromeda is the human soul and Perseus is Christ. The theme embodied by the fable, the salvation of the soul by Divine Grace, is a serious one.[17] The phrases individually are admirable, and they are admirable in all their interrelations save in those which are metrical. The poem is basically iambic pentameter; it employs a certain number of dissyllabic sprung feet, or spondees, of the type used by Googe and Nashe, and these work fairly well in themselves, although there seems to be no overwhelming occasion for them. The main trouble is this: that Hopkins employs extremely violent enjambement in three places—lines two and three, lines seven and eight, lines twelve and thirteen—without the rhetorical and rhythmic structure to support it. The poem lacks his usual violence of rhythm, which results, when well managed, in a steady rhythmic flow from beginning to end, a flow which minimizes line-endings; and it lacks the absolutely smooth rhythm and the long and intricate sentence of Milton, which likewise reduce the importance of line-endings. The poem employs elements from both methods which do not combine well, and the rhythmical (and hence the rhetorical) result is rough and jerky.

Inversnaid is a descriptive poem which pretends to be nothing else; it is beautifully executed; the meter is accentual, but the accents are real and not artificial, in spite of the fact that Hopkins feels called upon to mark a few of them. It is a minor poem, but a fine one, in spite of the obscurity in line eight.

The Blessed Virgin Compared to the Air We Breathe is a poem in which syllabic meter is managed with great success, and much of it is fine in other respects. I would make two fairly serious objections to it: lines 73 to 113 could very profitably be cut out, for they state nothing of the theme which is not stated elsewhere, and, although they are not bad, they are not as good as the rest of the poem and merely give the impression which we so often have of Hopkins that the poet simply did not know when to stop talking; and the expression *wild air* which recurs several times strikes me as very curiously in discord with the subject of Mary and her function:

> Stir in my ears, speak there,
> Of God's love, O live air,
> Of patience, penance, prayer:
> World-mothering air, air wild,
> Wound with thee, in thee isled,
> Fold home, fast hold thy child.

The expression *live air* is a fine stroke, but the concept of wildness is incomprehensible in such a context. One has the feeling that Hopkins somehow felt that one must be wild to be alive.

Carrion Comfort is one of the so-called "terrible sonnets" which were written during the period of greatest stress in Hopkins' career; it immediately precedes the sonnet beginning "No worst, there is none," which I have already discussed in the first section of this essay. *Carrion Comfort* is more explicit in one respect than is the other, for it states plainly that the anguish in question is imposed upon the poet by God in order to purify him, that it takes the form of his wish to flee from God and his inability to do so. The import of the struggle with God, however, is still remarkably uncertain. Is it, for example, the poet's lower nature which is in rebellion? Is he tortured with theological doubts? Or is he merely unable to face the appalling vision of God which his theological convictions would naturally give him? The poem could be made a far more powerful thing if couched in more precise intellectual terms, if the motive were rendered in the strong and orderly development which we find in Jonson and Herbert. As it stands, it contains a large element of loose emotion and is unsatisfactory unless one merely enjoys emotional indulgence for its own sake. The meter is looser than that of *No Worst,* and (no doubt in order to communicate emotional violence) meter and sentence-form alike become short, hard, over-emphatic, and monotonous in the sestet; and in the sestet also he twice falls into his trick of the mechanical repetition of sound and form which mars so much of his work and is quite as definitely a mannerism in Hopkins as in Swinburne. In *Spelt from Sibyl's Leaves,* for example, we get such phrases as *Disremembering, dismembering,* and *skeined, stained, veined;* and here we get *that toil, that coil,* and at the end the melodramatic (*my God!*) *my God,* which, though it has been greatly admired, leaves me, I confess, quite cold.[18]

In *To seem the stranger lies my lot* the theme is clearly stated, or perhaps one should say the themes: in the first quatrain the poet refers to the separation from his family resulting from his religion; in the second quatrain he refers to the separation from England resulting from the same cause, but adds that the cause is worth the expense. In the sestet he adds that he is still further removed from all that he loves personally as a result of his being in Ireland, but says he can still both give and get love; and he then complains bitterly of his frustration as an artist. The last matter is not clearly related to the others, though all represent aspects of his personal unhappiness and are thus in some measure related. The chief flaw in the poem occurs in the last line and is a matter of diction; moreover, it is so grotesque as to be ruinous:

> This to hoard unheard,
> Heard unheeded, leaves me a lonely began.

One can perhaps pass over the minor clumsiness to be found in the second quatrain of this poem, but a passage like this one is hard to endure. The mere fact that the author has genius is insufficient justification: there are many authors with genius, and many of these have greater skill and more artistic conscience than Hopkins ordinarily exhibits.

I wake and feel the fell of dark, not day states in the first quatrain the theme of spiritual agony which we have seen in other poems. In the second quatrain, by way of a comparison, it is suggested that this agony may be in part the result of separation from

149

a friend and hence of personal loneliness. The sestet states that the condition is the result of the poet's realization of the limitations of his own identity, yet the nature of the limitations is not given, and the explicit theme hardly seems an adequate account of feelings so violent. The poem is one of the best of this group; it is relatively unmarred by stylistic eccentricities. Its chief fault in the matter of style is a certain hard, emphatic, and monotonous rhythm, a rhythm common in Hopkins, and somewhat mechanical and imperceptive.

Patience, hard thing is one of the best sonnets also, and I think better than the last. The poem is a generalized statement rather than a personal one, and the poet is freed for the moment from his somewhat obscure emotions; the poem is genuinely moving, yet it has not the concentration and precision which one finds in the greatest poetry, but is somehow a little blurred. The third and fourth lines, for example, get their effect, such as it is, by the familiar devices of quick repetition and alliteration, not by the force of any particular phrase or series of phrases, and the two sensory images, of the ivy and of the honeycomb, although the former at any rate is charming, are scarcely necessary or up to their subject. Both of these images dull the meaning instead of sharpening it, distract the attention instead of focussing it, and the second in particular seems forced: the adjective *crisp,* for example, although it describes a real honeycomb is irrelevant to the idea and interrupts the poem.

My own heart let me more have pity on is another poem of unclarified emotion, and is one of the weakest: it is little more than a collection of mannerisms, a game of alliteration and other phonetic repetitions, and the diction and grammar of the last two lines are grotesque and clumsy.

In Honour of St. Alphonsus Rodriguez I think the best of Hopkins' sonnets and one of his five best poems. It is marred by the expression *gashed flesh or galled shield* in the second line: the difficulty is not merely one of alliteration, but of difficult consonant combinations and excessive length of syllables, so that the phrase is hard to pronounce and receives a forced emphasis; and since the phrases are not very sharply perceptive, one feels, as one does so often in reading Hopkins, that emphasis has been made a substitute for precision. The phrase is a kind of habitual hold-over from his poems in the more violent meter and rhetoric and is out of place here, for the poem is quietly written. Hopkins is able here, as in a few other poems, to free himself from his obscure personal emotions, for he is writing of another man and of one very different from himself. The poem is not developed by means of a description and application, nor by means of the repetition of ornament. It is reasoned from beginning to end, and nothing is superfluous; and the simile in the first half of the sestet is not only precisely applicable to the theme but is beautifully managed in itself.

Thou are indeed just, Lord and *To R.B.* are on a single topic, the poet's artistic sterility, and they are about equally disappointing. In the former, when the poet arrives at the statement about the "sots and thralls of lust," a statement which conceivably might have been developed further with strong effect, he merely drops the matter and goes into a trivial passage about the banks and braes; the birds and blossoms which he describes here are outside of the moral order and are irrelevant to the problem which he has posed. The poem ends with a sexual image and a vegetation image in somewhat curious conjunction; neither is particularly good in itself and neither is particularly appropriate to the theme; both are trite. The sonnet *To R.B.* is better, but Hopkins shows his characteristically poor judgment in the use of sexual imagery. The mind of the poet (who is a man) becomes a mother; the nature of the sexual act, or rather the psychological state accompanying it, is profoundly unlike the state which he is describing; the nine years of pregnancy are grotesque. The second line contains enough descriptive realism so that it can ill afford its large element of unreality; and I doubt that Hopkins knew the nature and function of a blowpipe, or, if he did, that he considered them. The last line of the sonnet is moving, especially in its cadence.

Of the remaining pieces which I have listed for consideration, *Moonrise* is merely a descriptive fragment, lovely in its fashion, but obviously unfinished; the other three, though published among the fragments, could pass for complete poems.

On a Piece of Music I have already discussed in connection with its theory of art; however, it deserves more detailed consideration. The first stanza praises the work of art for the integration of its parts, and the mind of the artist for his power. The second stanza tells us that not even angelic insight, however, can enable us to judge the heart of the artist from his work, since artistic law and the nature of man are distinct from each other. I confess that my interpretation of the latter half of this stanza is more than a little uncertain, but the lines are more than a little obscure, and this is the best that I can do with them; my interpretation seems to fit fairly well into the remainder of the argument. In stanza three we are told that we can judge the worth of the man accordingly as he serves God, or not, and takes the side of right or wrong. Stanza four states the orthodox view that Good is Being, and that Evil is the privation of Being; good is everywhere in some degree, but there are many degrees of it, and since one is forced to choose, one should make the right choice in any situation, should choose the greater good rather than the lesser, and this involves choosing God as a chieftain. In the fifth stanza, we are told that the artist indicated his powers in the work, but only crudely; since the work has already been praised and will be praised again, this appears to indicate a general proposition that the work of art is a very inferior manifestation of the mind of the artist. This I find to be a curious and unsatisfactory view, for although from one point of view the individual soul is doubtless more important than any one of its creations, nevertheless it is in the work of art that the soul has its best opportunity to function with some approach to perfection. In the next two stanzas the poet states that the artist was not absolutely free but had to operate within the limitations of his own nature. The word *therefore,* which introduces the last two stanzas, may seem to refer to the stanzas immediately preceding, in which case a deterministic doctrine would be indicated in those stanzas. I think, however, that there is no such doctrine there, and that the connective refers to the whole argument as thus far given, or to a stanza of summary, unwritten but implied, and just preceding it. Such a stanza would make some such statement as this: we have seen that man as man is a part of the

152

moral order, but that his works of art, no matter how beautiful they may be, give no inkling of his moral nature and are thus inferior to the man himself. *Therefore*, say these last two stanzas, art is outside of the moral order and is merely a minor though beautiful end in itself. The poem is a curiously repellant affair as far as I am concerned: it offers a view of art which seems to me not only untrue but unworthy of a serious artist, and it accepts this view, especially in the last two stanzas, with a kind of enthusiasm which I find very strange—it is almost as if the poet were taking a lyrical flight into irresponsibility for pure love of irresponsibility. The best writing is probably in the fourth stanza; the style in general is not as clear as it should be, with regard to the expression both of thought and of perception.

Thee God, I come from misses being a remarkable poem by an inversion of Hopkins' usual procedure: instead of over-emotionalizing his subject, he treats it almost playfully; there are several passages which put one in mind of *A Child's Garden of Verses*.

To him who ever thought with love of me is a fine poem and could well stand among the best minor devotional poems of the seventeenth century.

On the basis of this short and incomplete survey, a survey, however, which is the outcome of more than thirty years' reading of Hopkins, it would appear that the most nearly successful poems are the following: *The Habit of Perfection, The Valley of the Elwy, Inversnaid, St. Alphonsus Rodriguez*, and *To him who ever thought with love of me*. Aside from these pieces one can find poems containing impressive phrases, lines, and even passages, but all of them marred, and marred seriously, by faults of conception and of execution. I believe that Hopkins is a poet who will find his most devout admirers among the young; at the age of eighteen I myself was among his most devout admirers, but my opinion has changed with the passage of time. The young as a matter of necessity do not know the best English poetry in sufficiently rich detail to be critical and are more likely to be impressed by novelty than by achievement; they are likely to be somewhat emotional and hence uncritical of emotion in others; they are likely to be given to self-pity at odd moments, and hence sympathetic with chronic self-pity in others. I am not one of those who find failure more impressive than success, though I realize that I am in a minority. I am convinced that Hopkins' reputation will rest ultimately on the five poems I have named, or chiefly upon them. The achievement is distinguished even though the number is small and the poems are minor. If one were to name the twelve or fourteen best British poets of the nineteenth century, Hopkins would certainly deserve a place among them, and I think his place will be permanent; but the place is not the place of the greatest nor even of one of the greatest.

FOOTNOTES

[1]The present essay was written shortly before W. H. Gardner's edition of the *Poems* appeared. Gardner includes more poems than do the earlier editions, and includes many new notes and markings from Hopkins' mss. On page 245 we get Hopkins' marking for *Woe, world-sorrow; on an age old anvil wince and sing.* Hopkins puts an accent over *world*. And over *sorrow; on an* he places a long loop which indicates that the four syllables should be read as one, and this unit carries no accent mark. I am unable to read the line in this fashion, and believe that my own marking does more for the poem.

[2]G. F. Lahey, *Gerard Manley Hopkins,* Oxford, 1930. pp. 103-4.

[3]*Ibid.,* p. 94.

[4]*Sprung Rhythm,* by Harold Whitehall, pp. 28-54 of *Gerard Manley Hopkins,* by the Kenyon Critics, New Directions, 1945.

[5]*Letters to Bridges,* p. 46. Arthur Mizener in *The Kenyon Critics,* p. 108.

[6]Arthur Mizener, *Ibid.,* p. 103.

[7]H. M. McLuhan, *Ibid.,* p. 19.

[8]We learn from a note on page 226 of Gardner that Hopkins had shaken goldfoil in mind. We do not learn how it was shaken. The ambiguity is still in the text of the poem, however, and the essential weakness of the image remains.

[9]McLuhan, in *The Kenyon Critics,* p. 27.

[10]Oxford University Press, 1942, p. 71.

[11]Op. cit., pp. 22-3.

¹²*Gerard Manley Hopkins*, by Eleanor Ruggles, W. W. Norton Co., Inc., 1944, p. 156.

¹³The version of *On a Piece of Music* discussed by Pick here and by myself later is from the Bridges and Williams editions. Gardner gives another version, longer and inferior. If the reader wishes to reconstruct the better version from the Gardner text, he should proceed as follows: strike out stanza 3 and the last two lines of the final stanza, and then read Gardner's stanzas in the following order: 1, 2, 6, 7, 10, 4, 5, 8, and 9.

¹⁴*Further Letters,* pp. 81-2.

¹⁵I am aware that one may find a few passages in Hopkins' prose which seem to refute these claims. Selma Jeanne Cohen, for example, in the Philological Quarterly for January, 1947, argues the opposite view. She cites a few passages from Hopkins in which he argues the need for "earnestness" and the perception of "truth." But neither in Hopkins nor in Miss Cohen is there any apparent realization of the need for implementing these generalizations, of establishing in detailed terms the way in which poetic form itself is related to the subject, is a means to the perception of truth in the subject. It is as if a politician should recommend good government, without offering a detailed program. It appears to be an empty generalization, offered sincerely, no doubt, but casually, and with no attempt to pursue its implications in a serious manner. Many of the passages cited by Miss Cohen seem to me to support my views rather than hers. She does not deal with the final stanzas of *On a Piece of Music* which quite obviously state the theory which Pick derives from them. And she does not study the poems: she starts with the assumption that the poems are both sound and great, and merely looks about elsewhere for theoretic justification of this postulate. In doing this, she follows the line of most academic (and perhaps other) criticism of Hopkins and other poets as well. Too much criticism proceeds in this fashion, whether it be criticism of Hopkins, of Poe, of Emerson, or of some one else. It is not criticism; it is apologetics; and it often leads to extremely untenable theories.

¹⁶*Gerard Manley Hopkins: A Critical Essay towards the Understanding of his Poetry,* by W. A. M. Peters, S.J. Oxford University Press, 1948.

¹⁷I somewhat innocently saw in this poem only what Hopkins

put there, but in Gardner (page 236) I learn that Andromeda is the Church of Christ (i.e., the Roman Church), *rock rude* is St. Peter, Perseus (as I suspected) is Christ, *wilder beast from the west,* "the new powers of Antichrist, which for G.M.H. would include rationalism, Darwinism, the new paganism of Swinburne and Whitman, possibly Nietsche." Gardner is doubtless right about Hopkins' intentions, but if he is right, then Hopkins is again at fault: this kind of private allusion is the mark of the cloistered amateur.

Furthermore, there are difficulties in this interpretation. Christ, it is true, founded his Church on Peter the Rock, but he did not bind her to the Rock in order to sacrifice her to the Antichrist; and, if he has to remove her from the Rock in order to save her, he will necessarily destroy her, for the doctrine of the Apostolic Succession will be destroyed, and there will be nothing left of the Church save some kind of Congregationalism.

[18]On page 245 of the Gardner edition we learn that (*my God!*) must be spoken in a horrified whisper.

Robert Frost

Or the Spiritual Drifter

as Poet

I.

Robert Frost is one of the most talented poets of our time, but I believe that his work is both overestimated and misunderstood; and it seems to me of the utmost importance that we should understand him with some accuracy. If we can arrive at a reasonably sound understanding of him, we can profit by his virtues without risk of acquiring his defects; and we may incidentally arrive at a better understanding of our present culture.

A popular poet is always a spectacle of some interest, for poetry in general is not popular; and when the popular poet is also within limits a distinguished poet, the spectacle is even more curious, for commonly it is bad poetry which is popular. When we encounter such a spectacle, we may be reasonably sure of finding certain social and historical reasons for the popularity. Frost is similar in his ways and attitudes and perceptions to a very large number of the more intelligent, if not the most intelligent, of his contemporaries: to the school teachers, the English professors, the more or less literate undergraduates, the journalists, and the casual readers of every class. These people are numerous and are in a position to perpetuate their ways and attitudes; this similarity, therefore, is worth examining.

Frost has been praised as a classical poet, but he is not classical in any sense which I can understand. Like many of his contemporaries, he is an Emersonian Romantic, although with certain mutings and modifications which I shall mention presently, and he has labeled himself as such with a good deal of care. He is a poet of the minor theme, the casual approach, and the discretely eccentric attitude. When a reader calls Frost a classical poet, he probably means that Frost strikes him as a "natural" poet, a poet who somehow resembles himself and his neighbors; but this is merely another way of saying that the reader feels a kinship to him and likes him easily. Classical literature is said to judge human experience with respect to the norm; but it does so with respect to the norm of what humanity ought to be, not with respect to the norm of what it happens to be in a particular place and time. The human average has never been admirable, and in certain cultures it has departed very far from the admirable; that is why in the great classical periods of literature we are likely to observe great works in tragedy and satire, the works of a Racine and a Molière, of a Shakespeare and a Jonson, works which deal in their respective ways with sharp deviations from the ideal norm; and that is why literature which glorifies the average is sentimental rather than classical.

Frost writes of rural subjects, and the American reader of our time has an affection for rural subjects which is partly the product of the Romantic sentimentalization of "nature," but which is partly also a nostalgic looking back to the rural life which predominated in this nation a generation or two ago; the rural life is somehow regarded as the truly American life. I have no objection to the poet's employing rural settings; but we should remember that it is the poet's business to evaluate human experience, and the rural setting is no more valuable for this purpose than any other or than no particular setting, and one could argue with some plausibility that an exclusive concentration on it may be limiting.

Frost early began his endeavor to make his style approximate as closely as possible the style of conversation, and this endeavor has added to his reputation: it has helped to make him seem "natural." But poetry is not conversation, and I see no reason why poetry should be called upon to imitate conversation. Conversation is the most careless and formless of human utterance; it is spontaneous and unrevised, and its vocabulary is commonly limited. Poetry is the most difficult form of human utterance; we revise poems carefully in order to make them more nearly perfect. The two forms of expression are extremes, they are not close to each other. We do not praise a violinist for playing as if he were improvising; we praise him for playing well. And when a man plays well or writes well, his audience must have intelligence, training, and patience in order to appreciate him. We do not understand difficult matters "naturally."

The business of the poet can be stated simply. The poet deals with human experience in words. Words are symbols of concepts, which have acquired connotation of feeling in addition to their denotation of concept. The poet, then, as a result of the very nature of his medium, must make a rational statement about an experience, and as rationality is a part of the medium, the ultimate value of the poem will depend in a fair measure on the soundness of the rationality: it is possible, of course, to reason badly, just as it is possible to reason well. But the poet is deliberately employing the connotative content of language as well as the denotative: so that what he must do is make a rational statement about an experience, at the same time employing his language in such a manner as to communicate the emotion which ought to be communicated by that rational understanding of the particular subject. In so far as he is able to do this, the poem will be good; in so far as the subject itself is important, the poem will be great. That is, a poem which merely describes a stone may be excellent but will certainly be minor; whereas a poem which deals with man's contemplation of death and eternity, or with a formative decision of some kind, may be great. It is possible, of course, that the stone may be treated in such a way that it symbolizes something greater than itself; but if this occurs, the poem is about something greater than the stone. The poet is valuable, therefore, in proportion to his ability to apprehend certain kinds of objective truth; in proportion as he is great, he will not resemble ourselves but will resemble what we ought to be. It becomes our business, then, to endeavor to resemble him, and this endeavor is not easy and for this reason few persons make it. Country conversation and colloquial charm are irrelevant to the real issue. The great poets, men like Ben Jonson and Fulke Greville, have few readers; though some of them, like Milton, are widely admired from a distance. But they offer us, in their best efforts, the finest understanding of human experience to which we have access; some people are able and willing to understand them, and the human intelligence, however precariously, is thus kept alive. If we set up false ideals of human nature, and our best poets judge experience in terms of them and so beguile us into doing likewise, the human intelligence is to that extent diminished.

161

Frost has said that Emerson is his favorite American poet, and he himself appears to be something of an Emersonian. Emerson was a Romantic pantheist: he identified God with the universe; he taught that impulse comes directly from God and should be obeyed, that through surrender to impulse we become one with God; he taught that reason is man-made and bungling and should be suppressed. In moral and aesthetic doctrine, Emerson was a relativist; his most thorough-going disciples in American literature were Walt Whitman and Hart Crane. In Frost, on the other hand, we find a disciple without Emerson's religious conviction: Frost believes in the rightness of impulse, but does not discuss the pantheistic doctrine which would give authority to impulse; as a result of his belief in impulse, he is of necessity a relativist, but his relativism, apparently since it derives from no intense religious conviction, has resulted mainly in ill-natured eccentricity and in increasing melancholy. He is an Emersonian who has become sceptical and uncertain without having reformed; and the scepticism and uncertainty do not appear to have been so much the result of thought as the result of the impact upon his sensibility of conflicting notions of his own era—they appear to be the result of his having taken the easy way and having drifted with the various currents of his time.

II.

I should like first of all to describe a few poems which deal with what in the hands of a more serious writer one could describe as the theme of moral choice. These poems throw more light on Frost as a whole, perhaps, than do any others, and they may serve as an introduction to his work. I have in mind especially three poems from *Mountain Interval*: the introductory piece entitled *The Road not Taken*, the post-scriptive piece entitled *The Sound of the Trees*, and the lyrical narrative called *The Hill-Wife*; and one poem from *A Further Range*: the poem entitled *The Bearer of Evil Tidings*. These poems all have a single theme: the whimsical, accidental, and incomprehensible nature of the formative decision; and I should like to point out that if one takes this view of the formative decision, one has cut oneself off from understanding most of human experience, for in these terms there is nothing to be understood—one can write of human experience with sentimental approval or with sentimental melancholy, but with little else.

The Road not Taken, for example, is the poem of a man whom one might fairly call a spiritual drifter; and a spiritual drifter is unlikely to have either the intelligence or the energy to become a major poet. Yet the poem has definite virtues, and these should not be overlooked. In the first place, spiritual drifters exist, they are real; and although their decisions may not be comprehensible, their predicament is comprehensible. The poem renders the experience of such a person, and renders the uncertain melancholy of his plight. Had Frost been a more intelligent man, he might have seen that the plight of the spiritual drifter was not inevitable, he might have judged it in the light of a more comprehensive wisdom. Had he done this, he might have written a greater poem. But his poem is good as far as it goes; the trouble is that it does not go far enough, it is incomplete, and it puts on the reader a burden of critical intelligence which ought to be borne by the poet. We are confronted with a similar critical problem when the Earl of Rochester writes remarkably beautiful poems to invite us to share in the pleasures of drunkenness. The pleasures of drunkenness are real—let no one delude himself on that score —and the Earl of Rochester is one of the most brilliant masters of English verse. But if the pleasures of drunkenness are regarded in what the sentimental critics are wont to term a true perspective, they are seen to be obstacles to other experiences of far greater value, and then they take on the appearance of temptations to sin. Dante would have dealt with these pleasures truly, placing them where they belong in the hierarchy of values; Rochester was not equal to the task, but Rochester gave us a fine evaluation of the experience of a man in his predicament as he himself sees it. He is like the demon defined by Aquinas: good in so far as he may be said to exist, but a demon in so far as his existence is incomplete. And like the demon he is also enticing, for he has more than usual powers of persuasion. We are protected against his incompleteness and against his enticements if we understand his limitations, and we can then profit by what he possesses; but without understanding, we may be drawn to emulate him, to form ourselves upon him—we may, in a sense, become possessed by an evil power which is great enough to control us and diminish our own being.

The comparison of Rochester to Frost is unjust in one respect, for Rochester was a consciously vicious man; whereas Robert Frost would not willingly injure anyone. Yet the comparison in other ways is just, for Frost, as I shall show, has willfully refrained from careful thinking and so is largely responsible for his own condition; and his condition is less dramatic and more easily shared by large numbers of his contemporaries than was the condition of Rochester, so that he is probably a greater menace to the general intelligence. Rochester knew himself to be a sinner, and he knew that he would be regarded as one. Frost by a process of devious evasions has convinced himself that he is a wise and virtuous man, and he is regarded as a kind of embodiment of human wisdom by hundreds of thousands of Americans from high school age to the brink of senility. He embodies a common delusion regarding human nature, and he is strongly reinforcing that delusion in the minds of his contemporaries.

The Sound of the Trees deals with a longing to depart which has never quite been realized. The trees

> are that which talks of going
> But never gets away.

The poem ends as follows:

> I shall make the reckless choice
> Some day when they are in voice
> And tossing so as to scare
> The white clouds over them on.
> I shall have less to say,
> But I shall be gone.

The poem has the same quality of uncertainty and incomprehension as *The Road not Taken;* it is written with about the same degree of success, with about the same charm, and with about the same quality of vague melancholy. In considering either of these poems, especially if one compares them even to minor works by sixteenth and seventeenth century masters, one will observe not only the limitations of intelligence which I have mentioned, but a quality, slight though it may be, of imprecision in the rendering of the detail and of the total attitude, which is the result of the limitations. Such a poem as Robert Herrick's *Night-Piece to Julia* is as sharp as a knife in comparison. Herrick knew exactly what he was saying and exactly what it was worth. Frost, on the other hand, is mistaking whimsical impulse for moral choice, and the blunder obscures his understanding and even leaves his mood uncertain with regard to the value of the whole business. He is vaguely afraid that he may be neither wrong nor right.

The Hill Wife is a less happy specimen than the poems just mentioned. It deals, not with a personal experience of the author, but with a dramatic situation seen from without; and the dramatic crisis is offered as something incomprehensible. The wife leaves her husband because she is lonely on their back-country farm, but there is no clear understanding of her motive; we are told that she is disturbed when the birds leave in the fall, and frightened by a casual tramp, and that a pine near the window obsesses her thoughts. The last section, characteristically entitled *The Impulse,* describes her final act as a sudden and unpremeditated one. The poem has an eery quality, like that of dream or of neurosis, but it has little else. As a study in human relationships, it amounts to nothing, and one has only to compare it to *Eros Turannos* by Robinson to discern its triviality. *The Bearer of Evil Tidings* deals with a similarly casual and sudden decision, although it is a more interesting poem. And one might mention also the poem from *A Witness Tree* entitled *A Serious Step Lightly Taken:* the serious step in question is merely the buying of a farm; but the title is characteristic, and the title implies approval and not disapproval—it implies that serious steps ought to be lightly taken. But if serious steps are to be lightly taken, then poetry, at least, is impoverished, and the poet can have very little to say. Most of the world's great poetry has had to do with serious steps seriously taken, and when the seriousness goes from life, it goes from poetry.

III.

I shall consider next some of the more clearly didactic poems, which will reinforce what I have been saying. I should perhaps mention briefly as one of these, a short lyric in *West-Running Brook*, a lyric called *Sand Dunes*, of which the clearly stated theme is the Emersonian notion that man can think better if he frees himself wholly from the past. The last poem in the same volume, at least as the volume originally appeared, is called *The Bear*. The poem compares the wild bear to the bear in a cage; the uncaged bear is a creature of free impulse and is compared by implication to man as he would be were he guided by impulse; and the caged bear is compared to rational man as he is. The poem is amusing on first reading, but it wears thin with time. The difficulty is this, that satirical poetry is a branch of didactic poetry, for whereas purely didactic poetry endeavors to convince directly, satirical poetry endeavors to convince indirectly by ridiculing what the poet takes to be a deviation from wisdom; and both forms depend rather obviously upon the soundness of the ideas which they expound or assume. Frost tells us in this poem that reasoning man is ridiculous because he appears to labor and to change his mind; and he implies that impulsive man would be a wiser and a nobler creature. The fact of the matter is, however, that impulsive man, if he is restrained, like Frost, by conventions and habits the nature and origins of which he does not understand, is likely to be merely confused, uncertain, and melancholy; and if he is not so restrained may degenerate to madness or to criminality. Within relatively recent years, we have had two tragic examples, in Hart Crane and in Ezra Pound, of what a man of genius can do to himself and to his work by energetically living the life of impulse. It is not foolish to change one's mind; one learns by

166

changing one's mind. Life is a process of revision in the interests of greater understanding, and it is by means of this process that men came down from the trees and out of the caves; and although civilization is very far from what it should be, nevertheless mankind has shown a marked improvement over the past ten thousand years. This improvement is the result of the fact that man is a rational animal, as I believe that a certain Greek once remarked. The uncaged bear, or the unreflective cave-man, is inferior to Thomas Aquinas and to Richard Hooker, to Dante and to Ben Jonson, and to assert the contrary is merely irresponsible foolishness. Frost then is satirizing the intelligent man from the point of view of the unintelligent; and the more often one reads the poem, the more obvious this fact becomes, and the more trivial the poem appears.

Frost expounds the same ideas more directly still in his poem *To a Thinker,* in *A Further Range.* The idea in this poem is the same as that in *The Bear,* but is even more plainly stated; we have the commonplace Romantic distrust of reason and trust in instinct. The poem ends as follows:

> So if you find you must repent
> From side to side in argument,
> At least don't use your mind too hard,
> But trust my instinct—I'm a bard.

The poem is badly written, but one couplet is momentarily amusing:

> I own I never really warmed
> To the reformer or reformed.

Yet when we examine it more carefully, there is something almost contemptible about it. There are, of course, reformers and reformers, and many of them have been ludicrous or worse. Frost is invoking the image of the soap-box politician or the street-corner preacher in order to discredit reason. But the word *reform* can be best evaluated if one separates the syllables for a moment. To reform means to re-form. And the progress of civilization has been a process of re-forming human nature. Socrates

167

re-formed the human mind; Jesus re-formed man's moral and religious nature; Aquinas re-formed philosophical method and content; and William the Silent re-formed the idea of the state. Frost endeavors to gain his point by sleight-of-hand: he endeavors to obscure the difference between St. Thomas Aquinas and Pussyfoot Johnson.

Even Frost, with his instinct to guide him, is not proof against wavering, however. In the same volume with the poem just described is a poem called *The White-Tailed Hornet,* in which Frost describes the activities of a hornet and the errors it commits under the guidance of instinct, and he reprehends mankind for having engaged in "downward comparisons":

> As long on earth
> As our comparisons were stoutly upward
> With gods and angels, we were men at least,
> But little lower than the gods and angels.
> But once comparisons were yielded downward,
> Once we began to see our images
> Reflected in the mud and even dust,
> 'Twas disillusion upon disillusion.
> We were lost piecemeal to the animals
> Like people thrown out to delay the wolves.

Yet we have seen Frost himself engaging in downward comparisons, and we shall see him doing it again. This is the only poem in Frost's works which seems to represent a conscious rejection of his usual ideas, and this poem, as I have said, even occurs in the same volume with the poem which I quoted previously, *To a Thinker.* It is possible that Frost shares the contempt felt by Emerson and by Whitman for consistency, or he may be so inexperienced a thinker as to be unaware of his inconsistency; the point is of little importance, for he nowhere else takes up this argument.

Frost has something to say of the relationship of the individual to society. His most extensive poem on this subject is called *Build Soil—A Political Pastoral,* and was delivered at Columbia University, May 31, 1932, before the national party conventions of that year. It will be remembered that these were the conventions which led to the first election of Franklin D. Roosevelt, and that the time was one of the darkest periods in the history of the nation. The poem is Frost's most ambitious effort to deal with his social, political, and economic views. As to his economic views, he says that if he were dictator of the country:

> I'd let things take their course
> And then I'd claim the credit for the outcome.

This statement, if it means anything at all, is a statement of belief in an unrestrained laissez-faire system, of the sort that Emerson would have approved; a belief that if things are left alone they must come right. It represents a doctrine of political drifting which corresponds to the doctrine of personal drifting which we have already seen; in practice, it could lead only to the withdrawal from public affairs of the citizen not concerned primarily with personal aggrandizement, and to the surrender of the nation to the unscrupulous go-getter, who, though he may not be a drifter, is not governed by admirable aims. It is similarly an obscurantistic doctrine: it implies that this realm of human activity, like others, cannot be dealt with rationally and is better if not understood. As to the behavior of the private citizen, Frost says:

> I bid you to a one-man revolution—
> The only revolution that is coming.
> We're too unseparate out among each other—
> With goods to sell and notions to impart. . . .
> We congregate embracing from distrust
> As much as love, and too close in to strike
> And so be very striking. Steal away
> The song says. Steal away and stay away.
> Don't join too many gangs. Join few if any.
> Join the United States and join the family—
> But not much in between unless a college. . . . .

The individual is thus advised against any kind of political activity in a time of national collapse. The difficulties of effectve political action are obvious; the English-speaking peoples have been struggling with the problems of constitutional government for centuries. But if the reality of the difficulties results in our stealing away from them, society will be taken over, as I have said, by the efficient scoundrels who are always ready to take over when everyone else abdicates. In a dictatorship by scoundrels, the Frosts and the Thoreaus, the amateur anarchists and village eccentrics, would find life somewhat more difficult than they have found it to date. Frost objects in the last passage to the commerce of minds, and he objects to it earlier in the poem:

> Suppose someone comes near me who in rate
> Of speech and thinking is so much my better
> I am imposed on, silenced and discouraged.
> Do I submit to being supplied by him
> As the more economical producer?
> No, I unostentatiously move off
> Far enough for my thought-flow to resume.

It does not occur to Frost that he might learn from his betters and improve himself; he can see only two possibilities in his relationship with them—he can be silenced by them or he can ignore them and proceed as before. There is the implication in this passage that his personal "thought-flow" is valuable merely because it is his own, that it should remain uncontaminated. He believes that the man and the nation equally will reach their fullest development through a kind of retreat to passivity, through letting things happen as they may with a minimum of influence from without.

The same sentimental dislike for society, for community of interest, can be found in the poem called *The Egg and the Machine,* a poem appended in the *Collected Poems* to the group called *West-Running Brook.* The poem tells of a Thoreau-like adventurer who is exasperated to encounter a railroad running through his favorite marsh. After a locomotive passes him, he proceeds to find a nestful of turtle eggs, and Frost writes:

> If there was one egg in it there were nine,
> Torpedo-like, with shell of gritty leather
> All packed in sand to wait the trump together.
> 'You'd better not disturb me any more,'
> He told the distance, 'I am armed for war.

170

The next machine that has the power to pass
Will get this plasm in its goggle-glass.'

Here are several familiar Romantic attitudes: resentment at being unable to achieve the absolute privacy which Frost names as a primary desideratum in *Build Soil,* the sentimental regard for the untouched wilderness (the untouched wilderness would provide absolute privacy for the unique Romantic), and the sentimental hatred for the machine. I am willing to admit, in connection with the last matter, that machinery is sometimes far from beautiful, both in itself and in some of its effects, but its benefits have been overwhelmingly great, and the literary farmer in Vermont could scarcely hope to subsist either as farmer or as writer without its help, any more than he could hope to subsist unless a good many people faced moral and political realities; and it is curiously unjust that the locomotive, that patient and innocuous draft horse of civilization, should be selected to symbolize the viciousness of machinery. Frost's real objection to the machine, I suspect, is its social nature; it requires and facilitates cooperation, and Frost is unwilling to recognize its respectability mainly for this reason.

There have been other literary works dealing with resentment at the machine and the changes it has introduced; the resentment I believe to be foolish, but in certain settings it may have a tragic if barbarous dignity. Bret Harte wrote a story called *Maruja,* which tells of the first railroad to proceed through the San Antonio Ranch in what is now Los Altos, California, and of the resentment of the old Indian overseer at this destruction of the old order. The Indian, Pereo, whose resentment against the incoming Anglo-Americans had developed to the point of paranoia, and who had murdered one of the newcomers by roping him about the neck from horseback and dragging him to death, rode out against the first locomotive, roped it, and tried to drag it from the tracks, and was himself dragged and killed. The negro ballad of John Henry tells of a "steel-driving man" who broke his back in the attempt to out-hammer a steam-drill. These actions are naïve and primitive, but they are heroic in a fashion, they at least have the

171

seriousness of honest violence. Frost's protagonist, however, expresses his feelings by threatening to throw a turtle-egg into the headlight of a locomotive. The turtle-egg, of course, may be intended as something more than a simple missile: it is "plasm," raw life, and hence capable of confounding (although only symbolically) the mechanical product of human reason. The trouble is again that the symbols will not stand inspection: the locomotive cannot be equated with human reason, for it is merely something created by human reason to facilitate higher activities; there is nothing either of wisdom or of greatness in the egg of a turtle; and the locomotive and human reason equally would be quite unperturbed by the egg of a turtle. As we pursue the symbolism, we are left where we began, with a petulant and self-righteous gesture, a feeble joke.

There is a kind of half dramatic, half didactic poem occasionally, of which I shall mention two examples: *West-Running Brook* and *A Masque of Reason*. The first of these is a brief affair in the form of a dialogue between a young husband and wife who apparently have just established themselves on a farm next to a brook which runs west instead of east; they observe a ripple in the brook, in which the water is thrown upward and apparently backward against the current. The husband comments upon the ripple in certain lines which are the chief part of the poem:

> Speaking of contraries, see how the brook
> In that white wave runs counter to itself.
> It is from that in water we were from
> Long, long before we were from any creature.
> Here we, in our impatience of the steps,
> Get back to the beginning of beginnings,
> The stream of everything that runs away. . . .
> It has this throwing backward on itself
> So that the fall of most of it is always
> Raising a little, sending up a little.
> Our life runs down in sending up the clock.
> The brook runs down in sending up our life.
> The sun runs down in sending up the brook.
> And there is something sending up the sun.

> It is this backward motion toward the source
> Against the stream that most we see ourselves in,
> The tribute of the current to the source.
> It is from this in nature we are from.

The theology of this passage, if we may call it theology, is tenuous and incomplete; it is what a certain kind of critic would call suggestive, rather than definitive; there is, in brief, very little to it. Frost seems to have suspected this, for he did not let his meditation on the ripple stand alone on its merits; he framed it in the dialogue I have mentioned and made his young people responsible for it. Yet the people are not depicted as characters, and their remarks lead to no dramatic action; the meditation gives the momentary illusion that the characters are more important than they are; the conversational framework gives the momentary illusion that the meditation is more important than it is. Thus the structure of the poem is actually a piece of deception, and the substance of the poem is negligible.

A Masque of Reason is the same kind of poem on a larger scale. The characters are God, the Devil, Job, and Job's wife. The scene is "A fair oasis in the purest desert"; the time is the Day of Judgment. Job and his wife suddenly discover the presence of the Burning Bush. She says:

> There's a strange light on everything today.
> Job: The myrrh tree gives it. Smell the rosin burning?
> The ornaments the Greek artificers
> Made for the Emperor Alexius,
> The Star of Bethlehem, the pomegranates,
> The birds, seem all on fire with Paradise.
> And hark, the gold enameled nightingales
> Are singing. Yes, and look, the Tree is troubled.
> Someone's caught in the branches.
> Wife: So there is.
> He can't get out.
> Job: He's loose! He's out!
> Wife: It's God.
> I'd know him by Blake's picture anywhere.
> Now what's he doing?

Job: Pitching throne, I guess.
        Here by our atoll.
Wife: Something Byzantine.
        (*The throne's a ply-wood flat, prefabricated,*
        That God pulls lightly upright on its hinges
        And stands beside, supporting it in place.)

This brief passage gives a clue to the nature of the whole poem.
Job's first speech above is a piece of remarkable rhetoric; there
is nothing else in the poem to equal it. It reminds one of Yeats,
especially of Yeats's brilliant but whimsical poem called *Sailing
to Byzantium.* From that passage onward, through the references
to Blake and to the plywood throne, we have details which are
offered merely for the shock of cleverness; the details are irrelevant to any theme discernible in the poem. Frost, the rustic real-
ist of *North of Boston,* appears in his old age as a standard exem-
plar of irresponsible Romantic irony, of the kind of irony that has
degenerated steadily from the moderately low level of Laforgue,
through Pound, Eliot, Cummings, and their younger imitators.
The method is employed throughout the poem.

The poem falls roughly into three parts. The first of these deals
with God's first explanation to Job of the treatment Job had been
accorded in life. God tells him:

                              You helped me
        Establish once for all the principle
        There's no connection man can reason out
        Between his just deserts and what he gets.
        Virtue may fail and wickedness succeed. . . .
        You realize by now the part you played
        To stultify the Deuteronomist
        And change the tenor of religious thought.
        My thanks are to you for releasing me
        From moral bondage to the human race.
        The only free will there at first was man's,
        Who could do good or evil as he chose.
        I had no choice but I must follow him
        With forfeits and rewards he understood—
        Unless I liked to suffer loss of worship.

174

> I had to prosper good and punish evil.
> You changed all that. You set me free to reign.

So far as the ideas in this passage are concerned, the passage belongs to the fideistic tradition of New England Calvinism; the ideas can be found in more than one passage in Jonathan Edwards, as well as elsewhere. The carefully flippant tone, however, is something else; it belongs to the tradition of Romantic irony which I have already mentioned, and is used to make the ideas seem trivial. The ideas and the tone together express the Romantic ennui or disillusionment which is born of spiritual laziness, the laziness which is justified by the Romantic doctrine that one can best apprehend the truth by intuition and without labor. One can find the same ennui, expressed in various ways, in Henry Adams, in Laforgue, in Eliot, and in scores of others.

The second passage of chief importance is the one in which God revises his explanation. Job insists that God's explanation is not the true one, that God is concealing something, and God makes the following admission:

> I'm going to tell Job why I tortured him
> And trust it won't be adding to the torture.
> I was just showing off to the Devil, Job,
> As is set forth in chapters One and Two.
> (*Job takes a few steps pacing.*) Do you mind?
> (*God eyes him anxiously.*)

Job: No. No, I mustn't.
> 'Twas human of You. I expected more
> Than I could understand and what I get
> Is almost less than I can understand.
> But I don't mind. Let's leave it as it stood.
> The point was it was none of my concern.
> I stick to that. But talk about confusion! . . . . .

The general idea is the same as in the preceding passage, but the debasement of the attitude toward the idea becomes now a matter of explicit statement as well as of stylistic tone. There is no understanding of good and evil in themselves, of the metaphysical questions involved. Good is submission to an anthropomorphic and undignified God and is made to seem preposterous. Evil is made equally preposterous, and for similar reasons. The poem resembles *The Bear*, but is on a larger scale. If these concepts of good and evil were the only concepts available, or if they were the best concepts available, then Frost's satire would be justified. But they are not, and in reading the poem one can only be appalled at Frost's willful ignorance, at his smug stupidity.

In spite of the close relationship between the two passages which I have quoted, however, the poem is far from unified. These two passages are separated by various outbursts of indignation on the part of Job's wife at the way female witches are treated, in spite of the fact that male prophets have always been received with honor; and there are other minor excursions. The concluding pages are devoted to the appearance of the Devil, who is called up by God, so that Job's wife may photograph the three main actors in the old drama as a memento. This passage is in itself an excursion from the main theme, but it is employed to permit subsidiary excursions:

> God: Don't *you* twit. He's unhappy. Church neglect
> And figurative use have pretty well
> Reduced him to a shadow of himself.
>
> Job's Wife: *That* explains why he's so diaphanous
> And easy to see through. But where's he off to?
> I thought there were to be festivities
> Of some kind. We could have charades.
>
> God: He has his business he must be about.
> Job mentioned him and so I brought him in
> More to give his reality its due
> Than anything.
>
> Job's Wife: He's very real to me
> And always will be. Please don't go. Stay, stay
> But to the evensong and having played
> Together we will go with you along.
> There are who won't have had enough of you
> If you go now. Look how he takes no steps!
> He isn't really going, yet he's leaving.
>
> Job: (*Who has been standing dazed with new ideas.*)
> He's on that tendency that like the Gulf Stream,
> Only of sand, not water, runs through here.

> It has a rate distinctly different
> From the surrounding desert; just today
> I stumbled over it and got tripped up.
Job's Wife: Oh, yes, that tendency! Oh, do come off it.
> Don't let it carry you away. I hate
> A tendency. The minute you get on one
> It seems to start right off accelerating. . . .

In this passage, the satire is aimed at the word *tendency,* but the exact meaning of the word is not clear: it may mean a trivial fashion; it may mean an intellectual movement; it may indicate that Frost is unable to distinguish between a trivial fashion and an intellectual movement, just as he is unable to differentiate among reformers. The mutilated fragment from Herrick serves no purpose, but is merely an aimless effort to be funny. The poem as a whole is at loose ends; no single part of it is intelligent or even tries to be intelligent. It is a curious performance to signalize the seventieth birthday of a poet of so great a reputation. It is matched in triviality and general ineptitude by the collection of short poems entitled *Steeple Bush* and published more recently.

The best of the didactic poems is the one called *The Lesson for Today.* The poem is for the most part a suavely satirical comment upon that school of contemporary criticism which holds that the modern poet is condemned to mediocrity because of the degeneracy of the age, and to this extent the poem is one with which it is hard not to sympathize. Frost addresses his hypothetical poet of the court of Charles the Great as follows:

> I can just hear you call your Palace class:
> Come learn the Latin Eheu for alas.
> You may not want to use it and you may.
> O paladins, the lesson for today
> Is how to be unhappy yet polite.
> And at the summons Roland, Olivier,
> And every sheepish paladin and peer,
> Being already more than proved in fight,
> Sits down in school to try if he can write
> Like Horace in the true Horatian vein,
> Yet like a Christian disciplined to bend

177

His mind to thinking always of the end.
Memento mori and obey the Lord.
Art and religion love the sombre chord.
Earth's a hard place in which to save the soul,
And could it be brought under state control,
So automatically we all were saved,
Its separateness from Heaven could be waived;
It might as well at once be kingdom-come.
(Perhaps it will be next millenium.)

From this subject, however, the poem wanders into a brief discussion of mortality in general and the poet's concern with the subject; and after that topic the poem closes on the poet's epitaph for himself:

I hold your doctrine of Memento Mori.
And were an epitaph to be my story
I'd have a short one ready for my own.
I would have written of me on my stone:
I had a lover's quarrel with the world.

These two transitions are casual rather than structural, and the poem falls badly apart. The last lines, moreover, are extremely bad. There is a weak sentimentality about them which one perceives easily, but the reason for which deserves mention. There are good reasons for quarreling with the world, or at least with large segments of it; much of the world is evil, and the evil had better be recognized and taken seriously. If the quarrel can be reduced to a lover's quarrel, it is not serious. It is as if one said to a murderer: "After all, you are human, and you have a perfect right to your own opinions, attitudes, and behavior; we are all human and should respect and admire each other." The principle back of the final line is vicious and corrupts the line. And the intellectual vagueness which is responsible for this week ending is responsible likewise for the fragmentary structure of the poem and for the weakness of the other poems which I have been considering.

Frost, as far as we have examined him, then, is a poet who holds the following views: he believes that impulse is trustworthy and reason contemptible, that formative decisions should be made casually and passively, that the individual should retreat from co-operative action with his kind, should retreat not to engage in intellectual activity but in order to protect himself from the contamination of outside influence, that affairs manage themselves for the best if left alone, that ideas of good and evil need not be taken very seriously. These views are sure to be a hindrance to self-development, and they effectually cut Frost off from any really profound understanding of human experience, whether political, moral, metaphysical, or religious. The result in the didactic poems is the perversity and incoherence of thought; the result in the narrative poems is either slightness of subject or a flat and uninteresting apprehension of the subject; the result in the symbolic lyrics is a disturbing dislocation between the descriptive surface, which is frequently lovely, and the ultimate meaning, which is usually sentimental and unacceptable. The result in nearly all the poems is a measure of carelessness in the style, sometimes small and sometimes great, but usually evident: the conversational manner will naturally suit a poet who takes all experience so casually, and it is only natural that the conversational manner should often become very conversational indeed.

It is worth while to mention one other poem in connection with Frost's retreat from the serious subject. The poem I have in mind is called *The Times Table*. The poem deals with a farmer who is given to commenting on death and who is reproved by Frost: Frost remarks that such comments should not be made

> Unless our purpose is doing harm,
> And then I know of no better way
> To close a road, abandon a farm,
> Reduce the births of the human race,
> And bring back nature in people's place.

We should remember that Frost is a poet and normally speaks with full consciousness of his role as poet; it is reasonable to assume that this poem applies to the poet as well as to other persons. The poet, then, should not deal with death or with comparably disturbing topics, because these topics distress and discourage peo-

179

ple. Yet I wish to point out that all people die, that human life is filled with tragedy, and that commonly the tragedies accumulate all but overwhelmingly toward the end. To ignore the tragic subject is to leave oneself unprepared for the tragic experience; it is likely to lead to disaster and collapse. It is the business of the poet, let me repeat, to understand his subjects, and as far as may be the most difficult and important subjects, in rational terms, and at the same time to communicate the feeling which ought to be communicated by that rational understanding. The great poet judges the tragic subject completely, that is, rationally and emotionally; the nature of the human mind is such that we can enter the poet's mind by way of his poem, if we are willing to make the effort, and share his judgment. In this way we may gain both understanding and strength, for the human mind is so made that it is capable of growth and of growth in part through its own self-directed effort. This is the virtue of poetry; in so far as it is good, and we understand both its goodness and its limitations, it enables us to achieve a more nearly perfect and comprehensive being, to reduce that margin of spiritual privation which is evil. But Frost advises us to turn away from serious topics, and for the greater part he confines himself to minor topics. The major topics impinge upon his personal experience, however, for after all they are unavoidable; but his treatment of them is usually whimsical, sentimental, and evasive; and in his latter years his poetry is more and more pervaded by an obscure melancholy which he can neither control nor understand.

IV.

Yet Frost has a genuine gift for writing, as I have pointed out, and this gift emerges more clearly in his later work than in his earlier, though still hesitantly and momentarily. The view of human nature which we have seen Frost to hold is one that must lead of necessity to a feeling that the individual man is small, lost, and unimportant in the midst of a vast and changing universe. This feeling is expressed in the well-known poem entitled *On Going Unnoticed*. The nostalgic love for the chaotic and the dream-like, which Frost inherits from the Romantic tradition, along with an habitual but unreasoned hesitancy or fear, which is the heritage of the earlier New England, keeps Frost looking two ways, unable to move decisively in either direction. He is neither a truly vigorous Romantic, such as Hart Crane, nor a truly reactionary Classicist, such as E. A. Robinson. He cannot decide whether to go or to stay, and the result is uncertainty and increasing melancholy. One may see the same difficulty in *Tree at My Window*. Frost sees his own mind as similar to the vague dream-head of the tree, the thing next most diffuse to cloud, and the feeling of the poem is one of a melancholy longing to share the dream-like experience more fully. One can trace the manner in which Frost has arrived at this state of mind, and to that extent the poem is comprehensible. The feeling appears to be rendered more or less truly; that is, it seems to be an acceptable version of the feelings of a man in this predicament. But the poet does not understand the nature or the limitations of the predicament; and to that extent the poem is incomplete and not quite sure of itself. Like *The Road not Taken* it puts on the reader a burden of critical intelligence which ought to have been born more fully by the poet; and if the reader is not capable of the necessary intelligence, the poem is likely to draw him into a similar state of mind.

The Last Mowing deals with the same subject, and even more beguilingly. It describes a meadow which is being abandoned and is about to be taken over by the wild flowers before the more massive wilderness moves in:

> The place for the moment is ours,
> For you, oh tumultuous flowers
> To go to waste and go wild in,
> All shapes and colors of flowers,
> I needn't call you by name.

The next to the last line of this poem—"All shapes and colors of flowers"—is a curious triumph of rhetoric. Shape and color are named as pure abstractions; no particular shape or color is given; and what we get is an image of the shapeless and the shadowy, of haunting confusion, of longing for something unrealizable, of the fields of asphodel. This poem in its subdued and melancholy, yet somehow violent, abandonment to chaos, is one of the most explicit statements of Frost's predicament, and one of the most moving of them. *Spring Pools,* from the same volume, appears to treat the same subject, but less clearly. In paraphrase, it is a warning to the summer woods not to drink up the pools of snow water and the flowers that grow from them—these flowery waters and these watery flowers—and organize them into something greater. It is a poem on the love for the small, the fleeting, and the elusive experience of the late Romantic; in this respect, and in respect to the extraordinary sensitivity of its execution, it reminds me strongly of a poem by Paul Verlaine: *Le Piano que baise une main frêle.* Superficially considered, the poem by Verlaine deals with a subject which is very different and more obviously decadent; but decadence is a state of mind, not a matter of the landscape which happens to provide the symbols, and in spiritual quality the two poems are remarkably similar.

The symbolic lyrics which I have been discussing are all to be found in the volume called *West-Running Brook,* the fifth collection. There is one poem in the volume, the sonnet entitled *Acquainted with the Night,* which surpasses any poem thus far mentioned and which seems to me one of the two or three best poems that Frost has written. Superficially, the poem deals with the feeling of loneliness which one has when walking late at night in a strange city; but symbolically it deals with the poet's loneliness in a strange and obscure world, and the clock which tells him that the time is neither wrong nor right is a symbol of the relativism which causes his melancholy. The understanding of his predicament appears to be greater in this poem than in most of the others; he knows, at least, that it is a predicament and realizes the state of mind to which it has brought him. In the seventh volume, *A Witness Tree,* there is an even more impressive piece entitled *The Most of It.* This poem represents a momentary insight into the vast and brute indifference of nature, the nature toward which Frost has cherished so sentimental a feeling through so many poems. For a moment the poet appears to be appalled. The poem deals with a protagonist who seems to have cultivated solitude, like Frost, and who heard only the echo of his own voice in the wilderness but who longed for a personal reply from nature. The reply, when it came, was not the one he had wanted. One morning he saw a splash on the far side of the lake, and something swimming toward him, and then:

> Instead of proving human when it neared
> And some one else additional to him,
> As a great buck it powerfully appeared,
> Pushing the crumpled water up ahead,
> And landed pouring like a waterfall,
> And stumbled through the rocks with horny tread,
> And forced the underbrush—and that was all.

Frost's buck has much the same kind of symbolic grandeur as the apocryphal beast in *The Second Coming,* by Yeats, and he has the advantage of greater reality; the style combines descriptive precision with great concentration of meaning and at the same time is wholly free from decoration, ineptitude, and other irrelevancy. The poem gives one some idea of how great a poet Frost might conceivably have been, had he been willing to use his mind instead of letting it wither. In this poem especially, and to some extent in *Acquainted with the Night,* the poet confronts his condition fairly and sees it for what it is, but the insight is momentary: he neither proceeds from this point to further understanding nor even manages to retain the realization that he has achieved. Much else in *A Witness Tree* is similar to the earlier work, and the next two books, *A Masque of Reason* (which I have described in some detail) and *Steeple Bush* are his feeblest and least serious efforts.

There are a few other poems in the later books, however, which are impressive, and they ought to be mentioned in justice to their author, although little would be gained from a detailed account of them. In *A Further Range* there is a moderately long lyric entitled *The Vindictives,* which deals with the looting of the Inca empire by the Spaniards, and with the way in which the Incas in return sacked their own country and buried the gold.

> One Inca prince on the rack,
> And late in his last hour alive,
> Told them in what lake to dive
> To seek what they seemed so to want.
> They dived and nothing was found.
> He told them to dive till they drowned.
> The whole fierce conquering pack
> Hunted and tortured and raged.
> There were suns of story and vaunt
> They searched for into Brazil
> Their tongues hanging out unassuaged.

This is probably the only poem in Frost in which one can find anything resembling heroic action; the poem is motivated by a simple and honest hatred of brutality and injustice so obvious that they cannot be overlooked. The hatred in question, however, can be justified only in certain ideas, the ideas of Christian and Classical philosophy, which, although they are a part of Frost's background and influence him to this extent, he has during all of his career neglected or explicitly maligned. The poem is a little loose in construction and is occasionally careless in style; but it has an honesty and a controlled violence which make it very impressive. In *A Witness Tree* there are several other fine but minor lyrics which stay in one's mind, especially *The Rabbit Hunter, Never Again Would Birds' Song Be the Same,* and *I Could Give All to Time. Come In* is a memorable lyric, but perhaps it contains too much of Frost's professional and somewhat sentimental charm.

In *A Witness Tree* there is a narrative of considerable interest, *The Discovery of the Madeiras.* It retells a story from Hackluyt about a pair of lovers who elope from England; the captain of their vessel, who had been a slaver, tells the man a singularly brutal story about the murder of a pair of negroes who were lovers; the man repeats it to his lady, and she withdraws to her cabin, becomes ill, and eventually dies. In style the poem resembles *The Vindictives,* but it has less force at its best and is often undistinguished. It is written in eight-syllable lines riming in couplets and has something of the effect of a modern and sophisticated ballad. But the best of the old border ballads differ in one important respect: they deal, commonly, with an important decision consciously made, and with the resultant action, which is frequently violent but which is also important, either for good or for evil; Frost's poem deals with the accidental impingement of a brutal fact upon a morbid sensibility and the collapse of the sensibility. Frost's poem to this extent is the product of a decadent state of mind. Frost runs up against another difficulty in this poem which he encounters in all his narratives: the virtual impossibility of writing a short and purely realistic narrative which shall attain great power. The narrative, if it is to be short, must be symbolical or allegorical, it must be packed with the power of generalization; if it is to be purely realistic, it must be developed and explored fully in its capacity as a particular history. The short story writer in prose meets the same difficulty, but the short story is a longer and freer form and so has a better chance of success; and furthermore it makes a more modest claim upon our expectations, so that we are less likely to trouble ourselves about its limits.

V.

These remarks have been unfair to Frost in certain respects. I have quoted most extensively from his didactic poems, and especially from those in blank verse. Frost is at his worst in didactic writing, in spite of his fondness for it: his ideas are impossible and his style is exceptionally shoddy. Furthermore, although Frost is frequently very skillful in the handling of short rimed forms, he is extremely inept in managing blank verse; in blank verse his theory of conversational style shows itself at its worst—the rhythms are undistinguished and are repetitious to the point of deadly monotony. But it is in these poems that Frost states his ideas most unmistakably, and it is necessary to understand the ideas to form an estimate of him at all. He is at his best, as regards style, in the short rimed lyric, but his short lyrics are less explicit in stating their themes, and unless one comes to them with a clear concept of Frost's principal themes one may overlook the themes or mistake them. Frost is at his best in such poems as *The Most of It* and *Acquainted with the Night,* in which he seems to be more or less aware of the untenability of his own position and to face his difficulty, or as *The Vindictives,* in which as the result of a fortunate accident of some kind he is able simply to ignore his usual themes and write as if he had never heard of them. The greater part of his really memorable work, however, is to be found among the symbolic lyrics, of which *The Last Mowing* and *Spring Pools* are excellent examples, lyrics in which the descriptive element is beautifully handled, in which the feeling is communicated with a sufficient degree of success to make them unforgettable but with so great a degree of imprecision as to make them curiously unsatisfactory. For the feeling does not arise merely from the contemplation of the natural objects described: if it did so, it would be too strong and too mysteriously elusive for its origins; the feeling arises mainly from the concepts of which the natural objects are the symbolic vehicles, and those concepts, as I have shown, are unacceptable, and when one tries to project them clearly into terms of human action are unimaginable. Frost's instinctualism, his nostalgia for dream and chaos, are merely the symptoms of sentimental obscurantism when, as in Frost's work, they are dealt with lightly and whimsically, but if taken seriously, as in the work of Crane and Pound, they may lead to more serious difficulties. They do not lead toward intelligence, no matter how far the individual devotee may travel in their company; they lead away from intelligence. They lead away from the true comprehension of human experience which makes for great, or even for successful, poetry. The element of the unimaginable, and hence of the imprecise, which lurks in the theme of *The Last Mowing,* will make it forever, and in spite of its real and extraordinary virtues, a very imperfectly successful poem; this poem simply will not stand comparison with such pieces, for example, as *Low Barometer,* by Robert Bridges, or as J. V. Cunningham's epigrams on Swift and on the calculus. *The Last Mowing* will for some years be a more popular poem than these, however, for, as I have said, Frost's confusion is similar to that of the public, and most readers of poetry still regard poetry as a vague emotional indulgence: they do not take poetry seriously and they dislike serious poetry.

Frost, then, may be described as a good poet in so far as he may be said to exist, but a dangerous influence in so far as his existence is incomplete. He is in no sense a great poet, but he is at times a distinguished and valuable poet. In order to evaluate his work and profit by it, however, we must understand him far better than he understands himself, and this fact indicates a very serious weakness in his talent. If we do not so understand him, his poetry is bound to reinforce some of the most dangerous tendencies of our time; his weakness is commonly mistaken for wisdom, his vague and sentimental feeling for profound emotion, as his reputation and the public honors accorded him plainly testify. He is the nearest thing we have to a poet laureate, a national poet; and this fact is evidence of the community of thought and feeling between Frost and a very large part of the American literary public. The principles which have saved some part of Frost's talent, the principles of Greek and Christian thought, are principles which are seldom openly defended and of which the implications and ramifications are understood by relatively few of our contemporaries, by Frost least of all; they operate upon Frost at a distance, through social inheritance, and he has done his best to adopt principles which are opposed to them. The principles which have hampered Frost's development, the principles of Emersonian and Thoreauistic Romanticism, are the principles which he has openly espoused, and they are widespread in our culture. Until we understand these last and the dangers inherent in them and so abandon them in favor of better, we are unlikely to produce many poets greater than Frost, although a few poets may have intelligence enough to work clear of such influences; and we are likely to deteriorate more or less rapidly both as individuals and as a nation.

English Literature

in the

Sixteenth Century

None of the books with which I am dealing[1] treats the Elizabethan drama; therefore I would like to begin with a few speculations on that topic, in order to get it out of the way. The Elizabethan (and Jacobean) drama has, I believe, been greatly over-rated. There have been two major reasons for this, the first of which may have induced the second. First, Shakespeare wrote at least three of the greatest tragedies known to us (*Macbeth, Hamlet,* and *Othello*), and a few others that are great as tragedies go; and there are great scenes and even acts elsewhere in his plays, notably in the histories. Shakespeare casts a long shadow: he learned something (not much, I think, in proportion to what he added) from his predecessors. His contemporaries and immediate successors learned from Shakespeare what little holds them more or less together, but they are thin in spite of what they were able to absorb. If we can imagine the whole body of dramatic work of the period without Shakespeare, and are willing to suppose for the sake of the argument that Shakespeare's contemporaries and successors would have been the same without him, I think it will be hard to defend the idea that we have here even a good second-rate dramatic literature. What we would see would be a body of primitive, though talented, drama (Kyd, Marlowe) and of decadent but equally unrealized drama following. Somewhere on the side would be the massively learned and theoretical figures of Chapman and Jonson, the second far better than the first, but neither a really successful dramatist. The second reason is that because the literature is bulky, has its fine moments, and exhibits the thought of the period, it has been a happy hunting ground for scholars in the history of ideas. A third and minor reason is Mr. Eliot's sentimental and semi-critical interest in the literature. But if we eliminate Shakespeare, we have no one to compare with Racine, Corneille, and Molière, and even Shakespeare is less competent than these men in many ways, though I grant that he is greater. And I doubt that we have anyone to compare even with Lope, Calderón, and Alarcón, though I have not read any large body of Spanish drama

191

in a good many years. It is a great pity that almost no scholars in the English Renaissance read Spanish, and that most read French so badly.[2] Without Shakespeare, the drama of the great period is a promising but half civilized medium.

The prose of the period is even worse, vastly inferior to the Spanish prose of the same period, for example, though some great minds forced their way through the barbarous medium without improving it greatly (Hooker is one, and Bacon another). If one compares the prose and the verse of the most remarkable men who used both mediums, such men as Gascoigne, Nashe, Sidney, Raleigh, and Greville, the difference is striking—and baffling. These men were highly civilized poets, but their prose, regardless of the value of the ideas expressed, is clumsy. Holzknecht's anthology gives us a passable cross-section of the prose, and so far as style is concerned, one cross-section is almost as good as another. Lyly is a relief when one comes to him, because his prose has a principle of order: the principle, like the matter, is trivial, but it is at least a principle. Lewis's treatment of the prose writers is in the main excellent, and he summarizes and criticizes content as well as style, but if one is interested primarily in the development of prose as a medium, one can learn more from *The Triumph of the English Language* by Richard Foster Jones[3] than one can from either Lewis or Holzknecht. Prose as a medium generally understood and usable began to emerge late in the seventeenth century, when the great tradition of the short poem was almost dead.

However, two mediums of expression were brought to a high point of achievement in the sixteenth century and were widely mastered, by minor artists as well as great, and were widely understood and appreciated: music and the short poem. With the first we have nothing to do on this occasion. Without counting pages, I should say that about half of Lewis's book deals with the short poem and with those forms of narrative and didactic poetry which seem to have profited in some measure from the developments in the short poem, and this is as it should be. But his treatment of the poetry raises certain questions as to his critical competence, the critical competence of professors generally, and the nature of literary history and historiography. The various kinds of short poem were handled in an expert manner by a large number of poets from Wyatt onward, the number increasing rapidly in the last twenty years of the century. Most of this work was minor, but some of it was very great, and by 1615 the foundations had been laid for the work of the seventeenth century and much of the greatest poetry of the Renaissance had been written. The whole subject would seem to have a certain interest.

The common way of treating the history of poetry in the universities is in terms of schools or movements. That is, one studies the Petrarchan qualities of the Petrarchans, the Metaphysical qualities of the Metaphysicals, and so on; or more narrowly the Sidneyishness of Sidney and the Donnishness of Donne. The qualities in question are real and they are a part of history: they should be studied. But when poetry is reduced to these qualities, the historian (and unwittingly the gentle reader) begins to think of poetry in terms of statistical averages, with unaccountable and violent revolutions from time to time: Sidney represents a violent break with early Elizabethan verse, Donne a revolution against Sidney and Spenser. There are a few revolutions in the history of English poetry, but there are fewer than the scholars believe. The worst aspect of this view of history, however, is this: it reduces the standard of any period to the average of the eccentricities of the period or school or poet in question, and leads to the neglect of the great poems which appear from generation to generation and hence to the neglect of the main line of development, that is, to the neglect of the facts which are the really essential facts of history.

One can see the results of this teaching in most of the young men who review poetry and criticism in our literary journals, young men who tend to be a trifle contemptuous of the academic world but who in the main are formed by it. In reading poetry they seem to be concerned not with whether the poetry is good but with whether it is of our century: and this means usually a very simple thing—does the poetry follow the mannerisms of one or more of the poets who are supposed to embody the intelligence (if that is the word for it) of our time, Pound, Eliot, Stevens,

Williams, or perhaps Miss Moore? The reviewer is helpless to identify honest writing, but he can easily fasten himself to a mannerism more or less in the way in which a barnacle fastens himself to a pile.

Let me list a minimal number of poets and poems: Wyatt (Whoso list to hunt, Tagus farewell, Is it possible, They flee from me, My lute awake); Gascoigne (Gascoigne's Woodmanship, The Lullaby of a Lover, Gascoigne's De Profundis, The Constancy of a Lover); Googe (Of Money, Coming Homeward out of Spain, To Dr. Bale); Raleigh (The Lie, The Passionate Man's Pilgrimage); Nashe (In Time of Pestilence, Autumn hath all); Fulke Greville (The world that all containes, All my senses, Farewell, Sweet Boy, Wrapt up O Lord, Down in the depth, Syon Lies Waste); Jonson (Though beauty be the mark of praise, False world, good night, Great and good God, Let it not your wonder move); Donne (Thou hast made me, At the round earth's imagined corners).[4] This tradition of the plain style, fairly sophisticated in Wyatt, less sophisticated in Googe and Gascoigne (but more powerful in Gascoigne), progressively more sophisticated in the later poets, leads directly into the best work of the seventeenth century. For examples: Edward Herbert (Elegy over a Tomb); George Herbert (Church Monuments); Henry Vaughan (To His Books, The Lamp); and others.

The Petrarchan movement, as we get it in Sidney and Spenser, is not the major issue of the last years of the century, as Lewis and others appear to think. It is a side issue, though a fairly important one. It contributed to the increase in sophistication, but the more able poets were not overwhelmed by the new rhetoric, and appear to have been aware of its dangers. The Petrarchan movement did not displace the tradition of the plain style, though it has obscured this style in the eyes of many modern scholars.[5] Nor, I think, can Donne be explained simply as a rebel against Sidney and the Sidneyizers: his more irritating work seems to be a parody of them, but the parody more often than not appears to be unintentional—a combination of his peculiar neuroses, his peculiar form of seriousness, and his very personal variety of bad taste; and his best work is in line with the main tradition before and after. The attempt to explain Renaissance poetry in terms of schools and revolutions results, I believe, in the neglect of the best poems and of the important historical facts.

But Lewis sees the sixteenth century in terms of two schools: the Drab and the Golden. He says that these two terms have no evaluative connotations; but of course they have such connotations, as everyone who has read the book has remarked. He would have done better to employ the terms of the age, to refer to the plain style and to the sugared or eloquent style: he would thus have come closer to seeing things as they were seen at the time and perhaps as they really were. He sees his "Drab" poets in terms of their dead mechanical jingling, and his "Golden" poets in terms of their sugared silliness. He dislikes the first and likes the second. He blames modern scholars for approaching the period with Romantic prejudices, but he sees the entire poetry of the period in terms of a Romantic prejudice: he likes the pretty so profoundly that he overlooks the serious. And he misses most of the best poems in both schools. The best poems in both schools have more in common with each other and less in common with their respective schools than have the typical poems; and this is the difficulty.

I will list a few particular objections, of various kinds—not all that have occurred to me, but some that have most bothered me. Lewis writes bitterly of the humanists. He says (p. 30): "The war between the humanists and the schoolmen was not a war between ideas: it was, on the the humanists' side, a war against ideas. It is a manifestation of the humanistic tendency to make eloquence the sole test of learning . . ." Yet on page 330 and elsewhere he praises Sidney for his eloquence, without regard to the facts that the passages which please him have little substance or seriousness and that the humanists are doubtless largely to be thanked for the dawning of this kind of eloquence. On page 227 he says: "But Wyatt's permanent value is to be found in his lyrics. They are not except in a very few places precursors of the Elizabethan lyric. A single line such as 'The erth hath wept to here my heavines' or a whole poem like 'The answer that ye made to me my dere' may look forward; but essentially Wyatt is doing

195

work of a different kind. His language is usually as plain as that of his English lyric predecessors; to a taste formed on the decorated tradition which runs through English poetry from Spenser to Tennyson it may even sound sub-poetical." Lewis does not want to admit that it sounds sub-poetical to him, but it does sound so: from Spenser onward he overlooks the great poems in the main tradition and concentrates—with real enthusiasm—on the decorative poems. And again (p. 235) he says of Surrey: "He does not warble woodnotes nor thunder in high astounding terms nor wanton in luscious imagery: when he reminds us of the Elizabethans at all, he reminds of 'well-languaged Daniel' or sober *Nosce Teipsum.*" God help us all! This might be Tennyson or Swinburne speaking, or, worse, one of their admirers. Of Wilson's *Rhetoric* he says: "To judge its essential merits as a handbook is not easy for us who do not know the art Wilson is teaching; I suspect rather than believe, it is not very good." And so on. Perhaps so, but its influence and the influence of other such books, even on the poets Lewis most admires, was considerable. For example, Douglas Peterson, in the Shakespeare Quarterly (V-4, Autumn 1954), has shown that Shakespeare's *The expense of spirit* is based solidly on a passage in Wilson, and one can find other examples of similar influence; and the rhetoricians were the descendents of the humanists. Lewis quotes a passage from Spenser (p. 390), which he dislikes, and labels it as "Drab," and then quotes a "Golden" passage:

> By this the Northerne wagoner had set
> His sevenfold teme behind the steadfast starre
> That was in Ocean waves yet never wet
> But firm is fixed and sendeth light from farre
> To all that in the wide deep wandering are. . . .

Of this he says: "That is plain gold; the unsubtle yet delicious flow, the frank (yet here not excessive) alliteration, the frequent images, the Homeric echoes." This from the man who brushes Raleigh off without mention of *The Lie* or *The Passionate Man's Pilgrimage,* who deals casually with Gascoigne, without mention of his *Woodmanship,* and who feels that Greville is a dull poet who in some undefined way may somewhat resemble the Augustans: Lewis simply has not discovered what poetry is. In any book of this scope there will be errors in scholarship, and if I had written the book I should doubtless have committed more than Lewis; furthermore, one can hardly expect that an Englishman of Lewis's age should have read an American scholar at least twenty years his junior. Yet had he read J. V. Cunningham's *Woe or Wonder*,[6] he would not have written this sentence (p. 19): "If Dryden departs from Aristotle to make 'admiration' the 'delight of serious plays', Minturno had led the way (*De Poeta* II)"; and had he read Cunningham's *"Essence" and the Phoenix and Turtle*,[7] he would not have floundered so helplessly in dealing with Shakespeares' poem.

There are many men who have read more in this field than I have, and Lewis is certainly one of them. Some of them will find errors in Lewis which I have overlooked. I have found more errors in my own few publications than I have found in Lewis. It is not the errors in scholarship which trouble me, primarily, however, for those are inevitable. It is the critical mind that bothers me. It is my own conviction that one cannot write the history of poetry unless one can find the best poems. The best poems are the essential facts from which the historian must proceed. The background of ideas is important; the characteristic eccentricities of schools and poets are part of the material; but without the best poems, the history is not a history but an impressionistic and perhaps (as in this case) a learned essay. Lewis cannot find the poems.

There is a great deal in Lewis's book which is valuable, and I may as well confess a great deal which has added to my own education. His discussion of ideas, his criticism of conventional dichotomies of ideas (especially in the early part of the volume), are very acute. And there is more. But what is the function of this kind of book? No single man is competent to write it. I recently asked one of my colleagues how many men, in his opinion, would read it through. He replied that very few would read it through, but that it would be used mainly for reference. He was probably right. But if it is used for that purpose it is misleading: it is the work of a man who has read most (perhaps all) of the literature

197

in the field, but who is competent to discuss only a small part of it professionally. One cannot understand and evaluate the book unless one has read most of the material discussed, and as far as reference is concerned, there are many books and articles of more limited scope which are far more helpful in connection with the matters which they treat. The book is, as I have said, misleading, and so is every other book of the kind which I have ever read. And within twenty years it will doubtless be superseded by another book on the same subject, which will be better in some ways and worse in others. The first-rate monograph, or the first-rate critical essay, is never superseded; it becomes a part of literature; but the text-book is a hugger-mugger affair, no matter who writes it. Lewis undertook a thankless task, and a hopeless one.

The two anthologies which I have been assigned are similar in their virtues and defects to Lewis's books. They represent statistical views, or cross-sections of the period. I have already said that I think this roughly adequate where the prose is concerned, but I may be wrong: I know far less about the prose than I know about the poetry. It is not adequate where the poetry is concerned. And the critical comments in McClure's book sink far below the level of Lewis; for example: "The Induction [to A Mirror for Magistrates] is rightly regarded as the best English poem between Chaucer and Spenser." This is what one might describe as a stone-age opinion, and there is little excuse for it.

Yet these anthologies are better than most. A good deal of traditional rubbish has been eliminated; a little new rubbish has been added; and (so far as the anthology of poetry is concerned) a good many great works have been omitted. These anthologies are designed for the college classroom rather than for the general reader (whoever he may be). I suspect that this kind of anthology is better for the general reader than the other kind, and perhaps better than Lewis's history, for we have here not merely some kind of historical and bibliographical introduction, but specimens as well. We meet, at least, a few pieces of the actual literature. We may get a second-rate opinion and selection of the literature, but we at least get something to read, along with some helpful hints, and we can go on from there. As to scholarship and criticism, one has to look for it wherever it happens to lie concealed. One tracks it down year by year, by employing the latest bibliographical methods. Or else one reads and reads and reads, and does one's best to remember. It is a messy business, any way one takes it; but it is also fascinating.

FOOTNOTES

[1]*English Literature in the Sixteenth Century,* by C. S. Lewis. Oxford University Press, 1954. This is Volume III of the Oxford History of English Literature, a projected series of twelve volumes by various authors. *Sixteenth Century English Poetry,* edited by Norman E. McClure; *Sixteenth Century English Prose,* edited by Karl J. Holzknecht; both published by Harper, and parts of a projected eight-volume series of anthologies under the editorship of Holzknecht.

[2]This remark is not directed at the gentlemen under review. Mr. Lewis appears to be a better linguist than I am, though I cannot guess as to his Spanish. Of the other two gentlemen I know nothing.

[3]*The Triumph of the English Language,* by Richard Foster Jones, Stanford University Press, 1953.

[4]This list could be greatly extended, partly by major poems, largely by minor poets and poems in the same tradition. I am now engaged in a critical and historical study of the short poem in English, in the course of which the list will be greatly extended. But this list will give an indication of what I have in mind if the reader has the curiosity to examine the poems. I have not listed poems which show objectively an influence of poem upon poem, but there are quite a few of these.

[5]At this point, I would like to interject one word of warning to the professors. Poets are not fools (I mean good poets); they are capable of perceiving in their early twenties facts which professors may or may not manage to perceive in their sixties or seventies. I am not trying to be insulting (the technical term, I think, is "arrogant"); I am trying rather to state an important truth which is overlooked for the greater part in the academic world. There is likely to be over long periods what one might

call an underground, or unpublicized, tradition of the best writing, which one can discover only if one has the perception to trace the tradition from poem to poem. I am fully aware that these remarks are heretical.

[6]*Woe or Wonder,* by J. V. Cunningham, University of Denver Press, 1951.

[7]*ELH,* Vol. 19, No. 4.